ACCULTURATION

ACCULTURATION

THE STUDY OF CULTURE CONTACT

BY

MELVILLE J. HERSKOVITS

PROFESSOR OF ANTHROPOLOGY
NORTHWESTERN UNIVERSITY

GLOUCESTER, MASS.

PETER SMITH

1958

Preface

The primary purpose of this book is to attempt to define and orient the study of culture contact by describing some of the work that has been done in analyzing the results of contact between peoples, and to suggest further research into the problems that arise from investigations of this kind. If it is concerned only with primitive peoples, this is not because it is held that the forces at work among primitive folk are different from those operative in contacts between literate peoples; but merely that the writer, as an anthropologist, has felt it to be the part of wisdom to discuss those data which fall in the field of his competence. Hence though we will here be primarily concerned with problems of anthropological research, it is none the less hoped that what is said will be of use to workers in other social sciences, especially to historians, sociologists and psychologists.

I am grateful to the Social Science Research Council for having made possible a period of reflection and reading on the problems discussed here that I needed to point the concepts that had been forming in my mind during the past years while working on Negro research—essentially an acculturation problem; and to my colleagues on the Council's sub-Committee on Acculturation, Dr. Ralph Linton and Dr. Robert Redfield, for the many stimulating discussions that helped further to clarify these problems; similarly, it is a pleasure to express my gratitude to Dr. Donald Young, who participated in many of these discussions. I am also indebted to Dr. George Herzog for bibliographic suggestions in the fields of music and linguistics.

Melville J. Herskovits

New York,
27 August 1937.

TABLE OF CONTENTS

I

THE PROBLEM

Intensive study of contact between peoples is a relatively recent development in the anthropological repertory, and is to be attributed to a constantly increasing interest in the dynamics of human life. In research having to do with human physical form, for example, analyses of racial mixture are taking their place at the side of those more conventional studies in classification whose aim is to describe and differentiate racial and sub-racial types. In an analagous manner, the attempt to understand the nature and operation of human civilizations through the study of "uncontaminated" primitive societies is having more and more to share its place in the attention of ethnologists with that other approach which frankly assumes that, since culture is constantly changing, a comprehensive program of research must recognize the value inherent in the study of peoples whose traditions have been or are today being influenced by the customs of other folk with whom they are in contact.

More resemblances than just this are to be seen between the present status of research in physical and cultural anthropology; in both fields, new modes of attack on old problems have forced students to a redistribution of methodological emphasis, while in both there also exists a certain confusion as to the ends to be sought, inasmuch as the problems of race crossing and culture contact are of such immediate concern that the demands of the practical situations to be met tend to obscure the scientific value of research of this kind. This book, however, will only deal with the effects of contact as they are operative in the field of culture. The biological aspects therefore may be passed by without further comment, except in such cases as that of the Eurasians of the Far East, or in certain aspects of contact between Negroes and Europeans in the New World, where the fusion of culture is intimately associated with the crossing of the physical types involved.

2

Despite recent emphasis on research among peoples whose cultures are in a state of flux, or where it can be historically determined that contact has produced a culture of multiple origins, recognition of the significance of this kind of data is nothing particularly new. The word *acculturation*, which best designates studies of this sort, has a respectable history, and by 1928 it had attained such ethnological currency that Webster's Unabridged Dictionary defined it as "the approximation of one human race or tribe to another in culture or arts by contact." This was revised in the most recent edition (1934) to read "the approximation of one social group of people to another in culture or arts by contact; the transfer of cultural elements from one social group of people to another" and, in addition to the adjective *accultural* listed earlier, the verb forms *acculturate* and *acculturize* were added—"to cause or induce a people to adopt the culture of another." In 1936 the New Standard Dictionary defined the term as "the imparting of culture by one people to another."

The word is still peculiarly American, however international the interest in the study of changing cultures may be; though it has been used by a few German students, the British have consistently preferred to employ the compound term "culture-contact."[1] This is recognized

[1] An exception to this statement is in Schapera, (1936).

by the editors of the New English Dictionary who, in their supplement of 1933, append the designation "U. S." to their definition—"the adoption and assimilation of an alien culture."

Some of the uses to which the word *acculturation* has been put may be examined, for they throw light on its meaning, and also document the statement that the concept is not a development of recent years. One of its earliest uses was by Powell, who in 1880 wrote "The force of acculturation under the overwhelming presence of millions has wrought great changes."[1] Six years later W. H. Holmes, in discussing Spanish Pueblo art, employed the word as a matter of course:

"The arts... pass from place to place and from people to people by a process of acculturation so that the peoples of unlike origin practise like arts, while those of like origin are found practising unlike arts."[2]

Powell later employed the term again and again, writing in one of his annual reports that the Bureau of American Ethnology had acquired specimens of "the arts and industries of the partially acculturized Papago Indians"[3]; and, in a popular article dealing with the future of the Indians, placing it in this context:

"...For such reasons the early methods devised for civilizing the Indian tribes largely failed....Progress was made to the extent that the Indians came in contact with civilized man and learned his ways and industries, but it was acculturation, not education, by which the advance was secured. The triumphs of civilization, the power of prosperity, the wonders of industrial art, all made a deep impression on the Indian and from them he learned much, but from the school and books he learned little."[4]

At about this time also, Boas, discussing the spread of folk-tales among the Indians of the North Pacific Coast wrote the following, in which the word is used in its current sense:

[1] p. 46.
[2] Holmes (1886), p. 266.
[3] Powell (1896), p. 44.
[4] Powell (1895), p. 627.

"The arts of the tribes of a large portion of the territory are so uniform, that it is almost impossible to discover the origin of even the most specialized forms of their productions inside of a wide expanse of territory. Acculturation of the various tribes has had the effect that the plane and the character of the culture of most of them is the same; in consequence of this we find also that myths travelled from tribe to tribe and that a large body of legends belongs to many in common."[1]

How rapidly the term had gained currency in the fifteen years following the first use of it is shown by its matter-of-fact inclusion in the columns of the Popular Science Monthly of 1895 by an anonymous writer reporting on scientific publications of the preceding month:

"*Similarities in Culture*—Prof. O. T. Mason closes a somewhat critical discussion of similarities in culture...with the conclusion that such similarities may arise through a common humanity, a common stress, and common attributes of Nature; through acculturation, or contact, commerce, borrowing, appropriating, between peoples in all degrees of kinship; and through common kinship, race, or nationality."[2]

Five years later, however, Powell used the word in a manner that has a turn of meaning somewhat different than the earlier uses of it by himself and others: "The process of culture ... is by invention and acculturation. The invention is at first individual, but when an invention is accepted and used by others it is accultural ..."[3]—a meaning that is the more interesting since the passage quoted occurs in a context of comment on the possible results of extended contact between various Indian tribes in pre-European times.

Ehrenreich (1905) was one of the earliest German students to take up the term. It is found in his discussion of South American mythology,

---

[1] Boas (1896), p. 1; see also pp. 9–11.
[2] Vol. xlvii (1895), p. 714.   [3] (1900), p. xxi.

where he speaks of the "areas of acculturation" (*Akkulturationsgebieten*) and "acculturational relationships" (*Akkulturationsverhältnis*) to be discerned in studying the myths of South American tribes. A more systematic treatment of the theme, but one that is entirely divorced from other than cursory supporting data, followed three years later when Vierkandt, in analyzing the processes of cultural change, devoted some attention to the phenomenon and its significance in the field of cultural dynamics. The discussion, not based on any field study of cultures where change was taking place or had occurred has, however, perhaps because of its deductive nature, quite failed to stimulate students to field research.[1]

In the United States, though the past decade or two have seen the word *acculturation* pass into the ethnological vocabulary, it has only been toward the latter part of this period that specific field studies of the results of cultural contact have been made.[2] Except for the studies recently instituted under the auspices of the Office of Indian Affairs, research of this kind has in this country been consistently directed toward the scientific analysis of cultural processes, in contradistinction to European investigation of cultural contact, which has with equal consistency been pointed toward practical concerns.[3] The significance of this for a clear understanding of the processes of acculturation that are occurring over the world is of the first order, and will be pointed out later when the difference between "practical anthropology" and the scientific study of acculturation is considered.

[1] The only German student who has made such a study, Wagner (1932, p. 60), speaks of Vierkandt's work as "in erster Linie theoretischer Natur," and discussing his concept of "indigenous" and "foreign" types of cultural change, says "An jedem realen Kulturwandel werden mehr oder weniger beide Formen beteiligt sein."

[2] Outstanding examples to the contrary are, of course, Mooney's papers on the Ghost Dance (1896). Radin (1913, 1914) also published two short papers on culture-contact among the Winnebago. These are commented on in the next section of this discussion.

[3] Cf. Mead (1932), p. 5.

3

It is evident that the students of cultural change who have employed the term acculturation have seldom sought to define it, or to assess its implications before using it—indeed, this is perhaps the primary reason for the present discussion. For some the word seems to imply the meaning inherent in its earliest uses—the result of somewhat close contact between peoples resulting in a give-and-take of their cultures; for others it appears to hold the significance implicit in Powell's usage of 1900—the process whereby a specific trait is ingested by a recipient culture; while still others apparently accept it as the means whereby an individual "becomes acculturated" to the patterns of his own society, a usage that makes the term "acculturation" a synonym for "education." Since all of these are but phases of cultural change, and in their psychological aspect equally involve the learning processes, it is not strange that in the minds of some students all these meanings seem to be held simultaneously, with the result that sometimes this concept of cultural contact appears to have one meaning for them, and at other times the word is employed in quite a different sense.[1]

It is of some importance, therefore, that the implications of the term "acculturation" be clarified at the outset before any further discussion of its meaning is attempted, and this can perhaps best be done by considering some definitions of the word which have recently been offered. "Acculturation," says Lesser in his discussion of the Pawnee Hand Game, ". . . is a useful term for the processes by which aspects of elements of two cultures mingle and merge."[2] Feeling that this definition is too broad, however, he qualifies it with the statement that acculturation must be distinguished from assimilation "as of a separate character," and then explains his meaning as follows:

[1] A striking instance of this is found in Bateson (1935), p. 179.
[2] Lesser (1933), p. ix.

"Acculturation may be taken to refer to the ways in which some cultural aspect is taken into a culture and adjusted and fitted to it. This implies some relative cultural equality between the giving and receiving cultures. Assimilation, however, is the process of transforming aspects of a conquered or engulfed culture into a status of relative adjustment to the form of the ruling culture. The problem of acculturation, when we are considering the American Indians in relation to their adjustment to European culture, is a problem of assimilation."[1]

He then refines the distinction drawn in the preceding passage by another qualification:

"In acculturation the cultural groups involved are in an essentially reciprocal relationship. Both give and take. As a result it is a valid problem to consider what is adopted and what not, and the whys and wherefores. In assimilation the tendency is for the ruling cultural group to enforce the adoption of certain externals, in terms of which superficial adjustment seems to be attained. The adopting culture is not in a position to choose."

Before analyzing this definition, we may quote from Parsons' introduction to her ethnographic study of Mitla, where the same terms are defined. It is perhaps unnecessary to point, in passing, how the quotation which follows, when compared with the passages just cited from Lesser, demonstrates the terminological confusion found among studies of this kind:

"In this book my task is to convey the insight which I got among the Zapoteca into the ways in which the traits of an old culture may perish or survive, and the traits of a new culture be adopted or rejected. For the most part, the analysis is concerned with acculturation, with what the Indian took from the Spaniard rather than with assimilation, which is a reciprocal process and would include

[1] *Loc. cit.*

consideration of what the early Spaniard took from the Indian in the development of both Spaniard and Indian into modern Mexican."[1]

The contradiction here is patent, for Parsons' implication that assimilation is a reciprocal relationship rules it out as applicable to just those situations where Lesser would employ the word; that is, where a group of people, in making their adjustments to a more powerful culture, take it over without in any appreciable degree themselves affecting the patterns of the donor culture.

The interchange specified in Lesser's statement makes it difficult to include under the rubric "acculturation" many of those situations found in the world at the present time as the result of the impact of European culture on native peoples. For Europe may influence very considerably the culture of an island in the South Seas, let us say, which can in no conceivable fashion reciprocate with any interchange,[2] yet there are few who would not consider these folk to be undergoing a process of acculturation. The case of the Indians discussed in Lesser's work is somewhat different, for there has been some interchange between them and the whites; yet, granting the fact that these Indians "have not met a culture of the same order of complexity or technical advancement" as their own, and that "in the methods which have been used to assimilate the Indian, neither technically nor collectively as tribal groups were the natives brought into direct contact with our culture as such," does this preclude us from classifying the resulting change in the culture of the Indians as acculturation?

The methodological principle implied by Lesser in differentiating acculturation from assimilation is one which, at best, can only be used with the greatest caution. For just when are a people free or not free to choose one or another aspect of a culture being forced on them by

---

[1] Parsons (1936), pp. xii–xiii.
[2] A recent instance of this is to be found in Firth (1937), *passim*, but especially Ch. II.

a dominating group? Does not the answer to this rest entirely with the judgment of the student who concerns himself with a particular case? In Lesser's own monograph, it is pointed out that the Pawnee, in their early contacts with white authority, were moved to a reservation from their aboriginal habitat with a consent on their part that obviously was but engendered by despair. Here they were taught agriculture, and they seem to have eagerly accepted the opportunity to become farmers and thus repair their damaged fortunes. That they did not succeed is aside from the point; the pertinent question is whether or not the invasion of their hunting patterns by this new technique—which was introduced by the whites, but which they willingly took over to the best of their ability—is acculturation or assimilation. Insofar as it was a free choice, it must be regarded in terms of Lesser's statement as the former; but in so far as it was imposed by a dominant power, it was assimilation.[1]

Thus while there is a distinction to be drawn between the two concepts, this cannot be accomplished under the terms set by Lesser, and by the same token, but for quite different reasons, the definitions advanced by Parsons must be equally subject to modification. For though the subjective element inherent in Lesser's approach does not enter into her application of the terms to Mexican culture, the differentiation of the two words on the basis of whether the borrowing involved in contact is a one-way phenomenon or represents an interchange is inadvisable.

The definition presented in an Outline on Acculturation published

---

[1] A further difficulty presented by Lesser's modification of his definition of acculturation is seen where he speaks of it as "the ways in which some cultural aspect is taken into a culture and adjusted and fitted to it," since he neglects to distinguish between the concepts of acculturation and diffusion. This point will be discussed shortly, but the question must here be asked whether diffusion can be thought of as anything but a process by means of which some aspect of a given culture is taken over by a group who previously did not have it.

by the Sub-Committee of the Social Science Research Council[1] may here also be subjected to scrutiny:

"Acculturation comprehends those phenomena which result when groups of individuals having different cultures come into continuous first-hand contact, with subsequent changes in the original cultural patterns of either or both groups."

To this definition a note is appended, which must be regarded as an integral part of it:

"Under this definition, acculturation is to be distinguished from *culture-change*, of which it is but one aspect, and *assimilation*, which is at times a phase of acculturation. It is also to be differentiated from *diffusion*, which, while occurring in all instances of acculturation, is not only a phenomenon which frequently takes place without the occurrence of the types of contact between peoples specified in the definition given above, but also constitutes only one aspect of the process of acculturation."

This definition is seen to rule out several interpretations of the word that have from time to time been made. It excludes the application of the term to the manner in which an individual acquires a working knowledge of the skills and traditional modes of thought of his own culture, which, as has been stated, would make "acculturation" synonymous with "education" as used in its broadest sense; it indicates that, because of the nature of the contact specified, the cultures concerned are taken over on a generous scale, and thus, by implication, excludes those situations where only a single aspect of a culture is transmitted; while, finally and most importantly, it is entirely colorless concerning the relative complexity of the two cultures involved, and whether one is dominated by the other or contact takes place on a plane of comparative equality. This definition

[1] Redfield, Linton, and Herskovits, (1936). This outline is reproduced as an appendix to the present study.

is likewise noncommittal as to whether an interchange of culture occurs between the two groups party to the contact, or whether the process is a matter of one of them borrowing from the other without any interchange at all resulting—if, indeed, this is ever possible. In addition, as the matter has been put: "It plainly does not differentiate contacts between historic and non-literate folk from those between two primitive peoples. Nor does it touch upon the motivations behind studies of these cultures . . ."[1]

One of the points in this definition to which objection must be raised is contained in the phrase "groups of individuals." It was because of this that, in explaining the method of a specific acculturation study, a statement of the approach used was phrased as follows: "Studies such as this, concerned with a people whose ascertainable past history shows the effect of first-hand, continued contact between two cultures, have in recent years come to be termed acculturation studies."[2]

The problems whether culture is an entity in its own right; whether it leads an objective existence of its own; whether it can be studied apart from its carriers; and whether it pursues its own way despite attempts to control it on the part of those who live under it are of considerable importance, and are, in fact, not altogether aside from the present discussion. For the moment, it can however be assumed that culture does not exist apart from human beings, and that where contact between cultures is mentioned a certain human contact must be taken for granted as the only means by which culture can spread from people to people or from generation to generation. Yet, while it is desirable to emphasize that culture is no mystical entity that can

---

[1] Herskovits (1937a), p. 259. This paper gives the setting of studies of acculturation insofar as this has to do with the specific approaches of the various schools of anthropological thought; and also indicates the value of acculturation studies in the general approaches to the understanding of culture.

[2] Herskovits (1937b), p. 323.

travel without its human carriers, it is also true that it is not a simple matter always to know when "groups of individuals" are in contact, as one assesses specific situations the world over where bodies of tradition have been or are continuously impinging on one another.

This is seen most plainly where the studies of secondary effects of contact, such as contra-acculturative movements, are made. It would be difficult to designate the Ghost Dance of the Indians of North America, for instance, as anything but a phenomenon of acculturation; yet, especially in earlier manifestations of this as analyzed by Spier, Gayton and others, the actual presence of groups of whites among the Indians is difficult to discern; while in Lesser's study of one phase of the Ghost Dance movement, it is the rôle of the Hand Game as affording the Indians a new interest in life and a point toward which they might direct this interest that is significant, rather than any incorporation of phases of the culture of the whites with whom they were, indeed, in "continuous first-hand contact." Or, the condition of the culture of the natives of such an island group as Tikopia, where certain elements of European culture, especially in the fields of material culture and religion, are today effecting an invasion of aboriginal patterns, may be taken as a case in point. Is the visit of the mission boat once or twice a year, and the work of a single missionary (a native of another island and not himself a European!) to be regarded as an acculturating force? Certainly this person is not a "group of individuals," nor can it well be maintained that recurring visits of those on the mission boat constitute "continuous" contact.

4

The problem of terminology with which we are presented may be simplified if the relationship between the words "acculturation," "diffusion" and "assimilation" be further analyzed. In his discussion of diffusion, Kroeber defines it as a "process ... by which elements or systems of culture are spread, by which an invention or a new institution adopted in one place is adopted in neighboring areas ... in some cases ... until it may spread over the whole world."[1] Diffusion, this process by means of which culture spreads in space, is contrasted by Kroeber with tradition, which represents the means by which a given culture persists in time; that is, the means by which the content of a culture is handed down from one generation to another within the same society. And though both of these "rest largely on the same psychological basis: imitation," yet "as a technical and ... semi-popular term" the word diffusion has "come to be nearly restricted to its intercultural meaning" so that one almost never speaks of the diffusion of culture from one generation to another, but only from one people to another.

"Assimilation," on the other hand, is defined as "... the name given to the process or processes by which peoples of diverse racial origins and different cultural heritages, occupying a common territory, achieve a cultural solidarity sufficient at least to achieve a national unity."[2] Its significance, we are told, lies deeper than the superficial adoption of similar traits of a common culture by a number of groups of different origin; fundamentally, assimilation is not achieved until a people have attained a unity of thought that underlies the "veneer" of acceptance of traits of a material nature. It is pointed out that there are "grades and grades" of assimilation, and that the process is not restricted to the historic cultures alone, but that in contacts between European and native societies, or between native cultures with one another, the repercussions of contact also involve the assimilation of the culture introduced by those to whom it has been presented.

That these three words do not have identical meanings, then, is obvious; it is equally apparent, however, that the significance of each

[1] Kroeber, (1931).
[2] Park, (1930).

tantalizingly overlaps the intent of the others. Yet the difficulty we have in distinguishing between these concepts is, in the last analysis, of no different order than that experienced by the taxonomist in distinguishing different units in the biological series. In the social sciences as well, differences of opinion must mark all attempts to define too closely terms which denote processes of cultural change as similar to one another as those labelled acculturation, diffusion, and assimilation. It would therefore be wisest to draw definitions that are more rather than less flexible, and not attempt to delimit the significance of each term too rigidly. The important fact is that these terms merely represent phases of a single process by means of which either isolated traditions or considerable blocs of custom are passed on by one human group to another; by means of which a people adapt themselves to what has been newly introduced and to the consequent reshuffling of their traditions as these were aligned before the new elements were presented.[1]

If this approach to the terminological problem be taken, then *in general*, diffusion can be thought of as that aspect of cultural change which includes the transmission of techniques, attitudes, concepts and points of view from one people to another; whether it be through the medium of a single individual or of a group, or whether the contact is brief or sustained. Now it is evidently useful for purposes of as-sorting different types of data, to distinguish *in this general field* those contacts which are brief and involve no prolonged association between an individual and folk of a different culture—as where, for example, a trait of Polynesian culture is taken over by a Melanesian group visited once by some voyagers from an island far removed—from those other types of diffusion that take place when a people are exposed over a long period of time to a culture different from their own. On the basis of the investigations into culture contact discussed

---

[1] Bartlett (1923), p. 136, has a similar point in mind when he differentiates between "transmission by contact" and "transmission by borrowing."

in the next section, as well as on the basis of research not reported
on there, it must be concluded that the term acculturation is best
applied to studies of this type; while the word assimilation can be
used to designate the process by means of which a synthesis of culture
is achieved, whatever the degree of contact or amount of borrowing.

Some further discussion of the difference between the concepts
of acculturation and diffusion may be profitable. For though both
represent aspects of the process of transmission of culture from one
group to another—with the difference that diffusion applies to all
such instances of transfer, while acculturation has to do with continuous
contact and hence implies a more comprehensive interchange between
two bodies of tradition—the term acculturation has further come to
be restricted to those situations of contact over which there is historic
control. And from the point of view of method, this is perhaps the
crux of the matter, for while conventional studies of diffusion have
assumed historic contact between peoples on the basis of the existence
of similar traits in their cultures, the nature of a given contact between
two folk, details of the manner in which it was achieved, and the
degree of its intensity are all beyond the power of the student to
establish.

Not so with acculturation. The historic contacts of the peoples
concerned are known and the problem is one of adequately applying
the historian's technique, of employing documentary materials, and of
gathering information in the field concerning the contact from those
who took part or are taking part in it. In this way the student insures
the accumulation of relevant information as to how long the contact
took place, or the circumstances that brought it about, and, in some
cases, even the character of the individuals who were instrumental
in influencing the changes that resulted.

This use of real history thus characterizes studies of acculturation,
rather than assumptions of historical contact based on reconstructions
made by working out distributional analyses. The advantages in

this use of historical data have been recognized by practically all those who study situations involving cultural change among primitive peoples whose past can in any measure be reached. This is the case whether these students are concerned, as are most of them, with an analysis of the effects of contact between natives and whites, or whether they are concerned with the contacts of native tribes with other natives; it is true whether their work is directed toward the ends of pure science, or whether they are primarily concerned with making more efficient the task of those who govern native peoples.

Thus Spier, commenting on the fact that "the problems of culture growth among primitive peoples can only rarely be answered at the hand of dated information," and employing the "dated information" available to him to analyze the Ghost Dance of 1870 among the Klamath, seems to regard this study as one of acculturation rather than of diffusion. "It is possible to discover something of the process of acculturation of this dance complex among the Klamath," he says in beginning the section where he analyzes his data as they bear on the problems he enunciates in his sentence quoted above.[1] Yet what is it that differentiates this work, or that distinguishes his more inclusive study of the same dance,[2] from his summary analysis of the Sun Dance which, in its various forms, is "diffused" among the Indians of the Plains?[3] Or, to take other examples from Africa, what is it that differentiates Schapera's consideration of the effect of European contact on the economic aspects of Kaffir life[4] from Torday's discussion of the influence of the ancient Kingdom of Kongo on the peoples of the interior?[5] Can it be said that the processes involved are of a different order? Or does the distinction lie in the fact that the contacts involved were different? The difference is only one of

[1] Spier (1927), pp. 45, 53.   [2] Spier, (1935).
[3] Spier (1921), especially the section pp. 500ff., entitled "Diffusion and Assimilation."
[4] Schapera, (1928).   [5] Torday, (1928).

the degree to which historicity can be established; in the first case of each instance cited, the history of the movement does not have to be reconstructed, while in the latter it must be conjectural.

The strategic value of employing known history in studying contacts between cultures, and the need to exploit this advantage is even admitted by those who commonly are most reluctant to allow any importance to an understanding of historical processes for students of culture, and who, in all cases, set their faces immovably against any type of historical reconstruction. Yet the exigencies of understanding African cultures, for example, where the contact between African and European peoples has been such an important factor in recent years, has caused those who take such an anti-historical position to recognize that in research of this kind the utilization of historical data is a *sine qua non*. The following passage may be quoted to make the point:

"Any anthropologist working in Africa at the moment is really experimenting with a new technique. Anthropological theory was evolved very largely in Oceania, where the relative isolation of small island communities provided something like 'typical' primitive social groups . . . The anthropologist who embarks for Africa has obviously to modify and adapt the guiding principles of field work from the start . . . He has to exchange his remote island for a territory where the natives are in constant contact with other tribes and races. More important still, he has arrived at a moment of dramatic and unprecedented change in tribal history. Melanesian societies, it is true, are having to adapt themselves slowly to contact with white civilisation, but most of the tribes of Africa are facing a social situation which is, in effect, a revolution."[1]

Such recognition of the flow of history in the study of a culture, and of the dynamic nature of the phenomenon, on the part of one whose anti-historical orientation is perhaps best shown by the disregard

[1] Richards (1935), p. 20.

of the history of anthropology found in the statement quoted, is also present in the writings of others who hold to a similar point of view. Indeed, the entire symposium on Methods of Study of Culture Contact[1] from which the quotation just cited is taken, is filled with point after point of emphasis on the need for recognizing the background of the changing societies being studied; while the need for reconstructing these cultures as they existed prior to the contact is not only admitted but stressed.[2]

5

Since the difference between research in acculturation and other approaches to the study of culture is one of degree rather than of kind, it follows that the field methods to be employed in acculturation studies are in the main those of any ethnographic research. There is, however, one special point of field technique that must be considered. For where European and native cultures under contact are being studied, the elements from the student's own culture tend to be taken more or less for granted by him. Hence this must be carefully guarded against lest the resulting ethnographic description be thrown badly out of focus.

The proper emphasis on this point has been well laid by Schapera in discussing those special aspects of ethnological method that apply to studies of the results of contact between Europeans and natives in South Africa.[3] Since "in any modern fieldwork," the task is "to obtain as full an account as possible of the existing tribal culture," he stresses the need of placing all parties to the scene in their proper perspective; that missionaries, traders, and administrators are as important as chiefs, sorcerers, and other native participants:

[1] *Africa*, vols. viii-x, *passim*. This symposium, in the main, consists of contributions by students of Malinowski, an analysis of whose papers on the subject of culture-contact, consisting mainly of discussions of the need for and methods to be used in studying the problems of "practical anthropology" is to be found in Herskovits, (1936).

[2] Mair (1934a), pp. 416ff.   [3] Schapera, (1935).

"This is easy enough to say. In practice it is sometimes difficult to apply, not so much because of technical obstacles as because of the outlook engendered by the training that most anthropologists receive before going into the field. If I may refer to my own experience, I found it difficult, when actually in the field, not to feel disappointed at having to study the religion of the Kxatla by sitting through an ordinary Dutch Reformed Church service, instead of watching a heathen sacrifice to the ancestral spirits; and I remember vividly how eagerly I tried to find traces of a worship that was in fact no longer being performed. And it seems so silly to record the details of a Christian wedding or confirmation ceremony with the same fidelity, let alone enthusiasm, with which one would note down the 'doctoring' of a garden or hut."[1]

All who have studied peoples undergoing acculturation, or folk whose customs have been subjected to acculturational processes and represent a blend of native and European or American customs, will testify to having experienced the same feeling. A similar methodological caution, taken from a study of the culture of Haiti, may also be cited to show how the same point of view was developed as a result of field experience there:

"In attitudes toward the gods, then, in the names of the gods themselves, in the manner in which they function in the lives of Haitians, and in the importance of the ceremonial connected with them, much of African tradition which has carried over into Haitian religious life has been retained in pure form. Yet the intrusion of Catholic custom into these African patterns—often noted, though generally in passing—also must be studied if the significance of the forms of Haitian folk-religion is to be grasped. That this aspect of *vodun* has received the scant attention it has had is probably to be ascribed to two causes. The first takes the Catholic element for granted, so that even where a particularly dramatic element of Catholic practice is seen in an African setting... specific mention is

[1] *Op. cit.*, p. 317.

made of this without attempting to dissect its historic or psycho-logical rôle. The second reason for the comparative disregard of Catholic influence is that for Europeans it is a commonplace. Spirit possession and sacrifices, African song and drum rhythms are more 'exciting' than prayers and hymns of the Church...."[1]

On his guard against thus taking the familiar for granted, the competent field-worker otherwise prosecutes his study of acculturation along lines of generally recognized methods of field procedure, and attempts to obtain as rounded a picture as possible of the culture he is studying in its present manifestations. This matter of the "rounded presentation" of a culture, whether under acculturation or in a relative state of stability, is, however, something that is more easily urged than achieved, as is to be seen from the field reports of those whose theoretical position is most insistent on the need for complete data on a culture before the interrelations of its various aspects can be dealt with adequately. For the task of describing the life of any group, when approached from the point of view of workable method, almost demands that the phenomena be classified within their separate categories both when field data are gathered and when they are published.

If such a procedure of breaking down a culture is not followed, especially where hybrid cultures or societies in a condition of flux due to pressure from an outside source are being studied, one of two things happens. In one approach, a single phase of the culture is treated so exhaustively in the attempt to pursue to the last point of association its relationship to all other aspects of the culture that, seen from the point of view of this single institution, this culture fails to yield a scientifically useful description of reality. The other, which is the more common, is that the student does not see the forest for the trees, so that a discussion of mythology tells us more of social organization than of the tales themselves, because myths are the sanctions underlying clan organization!

[1] Herskovits (1937b), pp. 270–271.

No one would deny so obvious a statement that all aspects of a culture are interrelated; students from the early days of anthropology have not failed to recognize this fact as presenting one of the most difficult of all problems in the preparation of data for the use of fellow-workers. The point that must especially be remembered, where work is being carried out in the confused situations with which the anthropologist who is concerned with acculturated folk must perforce deal, is that certain working norms regarding the presentation of data that have been, and probably will in the future be found best adapted to the task of the ethnologist in reporting on the cultures he studies, can be held to with advantage even where the "rounded" presentation of the life of a people is, as it should be, the aim in view. Economics has quite naturally its ritualistic and magical basis in many primitive societies; nor does any competent student overlook the fact that the lore of a people, to be living, must function in some manner that makes it valid for that people.

But if we are to understand the life of any folk, it is essential to organize the data in a form that permits us to know the patterning of their conduct, or, in psychological terms, those consenses of individual behavior patterns that permit the student of culture to differentiate one civilization from another. And granting the validity of the position which holds that:

"...culture is not merely a system of formal practices and beliefs. It is made up essentially of individual reactions to and variations from a traditionally standardised pattern; and, indeed, no culture can ever be understood unless special attention is paid to this range of individual manifestations..."[1]

yet, as the author of this passage himself has clearly demonstrated in his own reports of fieldwork, it follows that to be able to cope with a degree of variation about a norm heightened by the incident of

[1] Schapera (1935), p. 319.

impact between two cultures, one must exercise the more care to present the norms of behavior as clearly as possible so that the significance of the variations about them can the more readily be grasped.

To put the matter somewhat differently, it is necessary to know the "style" of a culture—which is merely another way of saying that we must know its patterning—in precisely the same way that the student of art must know the styles that characterize the various periods of art-history in order to cope with the individual variations that are examplified in the works of artists of a given epoch. It is on this basis alone that an intensive analysis of the changing modes of painting can be made, and it is in precisely this way that the ethnologist must establish a basis from which he, or others, can make further studies into specific aspects of a culture. The rounded presentation, which holds the several sub-divisions of culture clearly in mind, must precede the detailed study of any phase of a specific culture. But it must be rounded in the sense that while it treats all of the subordinate patterns within the several large divisions of culture so as to give a sense of the fullness of the life of a people, it must not strain too much to integrate all aspects with each other lest confusion also result. Because some emphasis has properly been placed on the interdependence of all aspects of culture, it does not follow that the independence of its principal phases should be forgotten. Religion can indeed be discussed without constant reference to social organization; economics without analyses of art.

This is especially to be kept in mind when gathering and presenting field materials from cultures in a state of flux. For here, as almost nowhere else, it is not only essential that a full portrayal be given of the situation as it exists, but one that is of the greatest clarity, for on this depends the measure of success that will later be achieved by the all-important succeeding steps of analyzing the results of cultural contact. And while a full presentation demands the understanding of all aspects of culture, a clear one is best achieved if treatment of the several subdivisions of culture, the recognition of the existence of which empirically developed out of the study of many civilizations, be not handicapped by an exclusive emphasis laid where those impinge one upon another.

6

Before such an analysis of the data can be undertaken, however, the historic control must be set up. This is done in two ways; by field study tending to reconstruct the life of the people as it was lived before the acculturative process set in, and by means of documentary evidence. Neither of these present any difficulties in method that are peculiar enough to the study of acculturation to merit extended discussion here. That quite workable reconstructions of tribal custom that no longer flourish can be achieved has apparently been difficult to comprehend by those who are committed to the method of intensive investigation of individual primitive societies as they operate in a condition of relative equilibrium. And it is perhaps understandable that those who hold that "uncontaminated" societies offer the sole valid material for studying culture are apprehensive of reconstructions of traditions which, in their fullness, exist but in the memory of those who lived in earlier times. That the "difficulties of studying the traditional native culture, which has largely become a thing of the past ..."[1]—as one writer on culture-contact puts it—should therefore be stressed by them is not only understandable, but has a certain cautionary value that should not be underestimated. Yet is the ethnological documentation of the "base-line" from which change in a given culture took its departure really as impossible as it would seem to those who take this point of view? Can we do no better in this important phase of our problem than the following passage would seem to indicate?

[1] Wagner (1936), p. 317.

"It is obvious that such a reconstruction can never have the same factual value as the results of direct observation. It will be of the same abstract, generalised type as all field-work results obtained by relying solely on the statements of informants and not checking them against data taken from actual practice. It will be lacking in the everyday detail which is an essential element to satisfactory fieldwork, and it will be subject not only to the inevitable distortion of memory, but to that of prejudice, sometimes in favour of the old order and sometimes against it. It will not give an accurate, a complete, or a dynamic picture of native life, and if such a reconstruction was presented as the sole result of a field study, it would have little value... Nevertheless it seems to me essential for this type of inquiry...."[1]

Happily, the difficulties in the way of obtaining reconstructions are in fact not as overwhelming as this passage would make them out to be. May it not be that this groping with what, for them, is a new problem in method, arises from a lack of knowledge of the techniques of American students who have worked with the dislocated cultures of Indian tribes, and have obtained highly satisfactory results, even where the conditions of native life are so broken as to test severely the ingenuity of the ethnographer? Whatever the case, it should be recognized that by means of a judicious employment of questions answered by a number of informants, and by balancing such material against reports of those who had contact with the tribe in the days of its cultural vigor and the findings of colleagues who have worked with related tribes, it is entirely possible to obtain workable descriptions of the antecedent patternings of cultures that today are only fragmentary —accounts which, moreover, can even attain the living quality of a field study of a tribe that at present has a relatively stable existence.[2]

---

[1] Mair (1934a), pp. 416–417.

[2] This is exemplified in any number of American monographs, of which Lowie's study of the Crow (1935) may be taken as an outstanding instance; the methodological discussion in the introduction (especially pp. xvii-xviii) is particularly germane to the point under consideration. Another example to be remarked,

The reconstruction thus obtained is the point of departure for a study of the effects of the impact on the culture under analysis of a foreign body of tradition whose results are at hand through observation of the contemporary mode of life.

Though the discussion of the necessity for obtaining reconstructions of the earlier life of a people has here followed that of the need for the description of their life as it is lived at present, there are cases where the wisest practice in the actual study of acculturation would seem to be to derive the base-line from which the changes developed first, and then, once equipped with the insight into past conditions, to obtain relevant data concerning the contemporary manner of living. Where such a course is followed, the evaluation of changes that have ocurred as a result of contact will be surer, and an understanding of the effect had by the forces operative in the situation of change more clear, than if the present-day culture is first studied without reference to the past. This has been emphatically true in studies of the New World Negroes, where, because of a disregard of African background, the real significance of many customs has been missed, important aspects of culture not readily revealed to the student have been overlooked, and erroneous conclusions drawn. Without laboring the point, it must be emphasized that the study of cultural change—or, for that matter, the study of culture as a whole—can not be attempted without a vivid sense of the historically dynamic nature of the phenomenon. Hence, the more background that is available, the better the treatment; or, conversely, and even more importantly, the less the sense of history, the more sterile the results.

That all actual historical documents bearing on a given situation

where a specific tribal institution of the past is presented in considerable detail, is found in McKern (1922). From the African scene, a well-balanced recognition of the possibilities inherent in reconstructions, as well as of the drawbacks of this mode of approach, is to be had in Schapera's paper to which reference has already been made (1935, pp. 321–322).

should be exhaustively analyzed goes without saying. Especially in the case of contact between European and non-European peoples will material of this sort prove important in indicating the manner and intensity of the contact, and, in some instances, even the types of persons who were influential in it. Information of this character has been neglected to a surprising degree, not only in studies of acculturation—where this is inexcusable—but also in studies of the ethnology of relatively undisturbed folk. Yet the light such materials shed on changing custom, the strictly ethnological data that they supply—since the early travellers were far keener observers than ethnologists generally credit them with having been—and the sense of sureness in time depth afforded, are of the greatest value in the study of any civilization, acculturated or not.

So important is it to have adequate data of this type that in the case of the contemporary culture of Mexico, where there is known hybridity of background, the unsatisfactory documentary evidence concerning the precise mode of contact between the Indian and Spanish peoples, and the lack of detail concerning the cultures which, several hundred years ago, were merged into present-day Mexican civilization, have made it seem preferable to some students to set up a series of categories of different degrees of exposure to the present-day outer world; and on this basis to analyze the differences between the people whose modes of life fit into such categories,[1] rather then to phrase research in terms of the integration of Spanish and Indian cultures into that of the Mexican today. To compare communities of the order of city, town, and village, and to express the differences between them "in terms of a process of transition" represents an attack on the problems of cultural change that has significance, and should both yield results of importance and stimulate investigators to new modes of approach elsewhere. In the sense of being research into the working out of processes of acculturation a long time removed

[1] Redfield, (1934).

from the original impulses, indeed, analyses of this type may well
be regarded as a profitable form for other acculturation studies. And
though the difficulties of employing historic sources in the Mexican
scene are stressed by some students who are interested in analyzing
the historical background of the present acculturated Mexican
societies more than by others,[1] and for the very reason that, "wisdom
in ethnology, as in life, consists in having more than one method of
approach,"[2] this approach well merits further utilization where it
can be applied.

7

With information concerning the historic setting of the contact
in hand, the cultures involved in the contact understood, and the
present body of traditions of the people described, the analysis of
these data may then proceed with profit along the lines suggested
in the Outline of the Sub-Committee on Acculturation of the Social
Science Research Council that has already been cited. The nature
of the contact, and the individuals concerned in it; the rôle these
persons played, and, if possible, the reasons why they exerted their
influence as they did; whether the contact was friendly or hostile,
and whether or not the two groups were similar or dissimilar in
numbers or in the forcefulness of their cultures: all these should be
pointed toward an understanding of both field data and the relevant
historical literature. Which cultural elements were accepted or, of
equal importance, those which were rejected, together with any
available information as to why they were accepted or rejected, should
also be exhaustively analyzed. Finally, viewing the culture under
investigation as a going concern, an inquiry into the provenience
of the elements of this culture, and the manner in which they are
integrated into the totality of the resulting culture will round out the

[1] Beals, (1936).
[2] Parsons (1936), p. 479.

presentation and, in making available an additional example of that type of cultural change that is called acculturation, will permit us to further our understanding of the processes of cultural dynamics in general.

One question that was raised as a result of the publication of this Outline on Acculturation—but one that is by no means only pertinent to acculturation studies—derives from the employment of the word "traits." Is it advisable, it is asked, in analyzing a culture that has been subjected to an acculturative process, to content oneself with what has been described as a "sorting-process into one of two pigeon-holes?" Do not facts treated in this manner "tend to remain discrete and non-comparable"; does not the "scholarly effort come to rest when the assignment to one heritage or the other has been made?"[1] Moreover, is it not also true that "assimilation is one of the most subtle and elusive of social processes, which does not reveal itself by plucked threads, by isolated facts ... ?"[2]

These points are well taken, for no ethnographic study which aims at being more than a tabulation of cultural items can rest with mere enumeration which, in the case of acculturation, takes the form of assigning to one source or another the specific elements in the present culture of a people who have undergone ascertainable contact. No type of ethnological investigation could be farther removed from that which employed the "classical" comparative method, or from the so-called "historical" schools of ethnological thought as exemplified in the generalizations about the contact of peoples made by the British and German diffusionist schools, than that which characterizes the study of acculturation. In a given culture, the assignment of one

[1] Redfield (1934), pp. 58, 61.
[2] Parsons (1936), p. xi. It may be remarked that Parsons' use of the word assimilation, that has been discussed above, does not for the present purpose lessen the relevance of the quotation, since its significance is quite that of acculturation in the present discussion.

element or another to a specific source merely clears the ground so that we can understand the kinds of things that were taken over or rejected, the ways in which they were integrated into the culture, and, from this and the study of many acculturative situations, of the possibility of working out general principles of cultural change.

As a matter of fact, this manner of treating cultures as composed of small pieces termed "traits" is more argued against than actually manifested in acculturation studies. If one goes through the literature, it is found that in no serious attempt to analyze such a situation has the student who has broken down the hybrid body of traditions with which he is concerned into elements, and assigned the various elements to their sources of origin, been content with this assignment of "traits." This is true whether the study is concerned with folk inhabiting the islands of Melanesia, or with peoples of the Philippines; whether it has to do with the Negroes of South Africa or the New World; whether it deals with broken cultures of Indians of the United States or the living cultures of Indians of Mexico. It is merely a step in method; and an essential step, be it said, if statements such as "in cultural contact, traits of material culture give way more readily than non-material ones" or "in a changing culture, women manifest greater conservatism than men," or any other generalization of this kind are to be investigated. But this is only another way of saying that the procedure is but a means to the end of understanding cultural change, which, whether among people where the historic contacts are ascertainable, or among those where they must be inferred, constitute one of the most important problems of the ethnologist.

8

In reading the published material on cultural contact and acculturation, one cannot but be impressed with the proportion of these discussions that are concerned with what has come to be called "practical" or "applied" anthropology. It is not the purpose of this discussion to assess the degree to which the resources of anthropology justify the application of anthropological knowledge to current problems, though this is a matter of some importance both in the realms of physical and cultural anthropology. Nor is it proposed here to discuss whether or not the scholar can exert effective influence in the face of those social and economic imponderables that are operative in most situations where the knowledge of anthropology might conceivably be put to practical use.[1] Here we can only consider the effects of these practical applications of ethnology on the scientific study of the processes of culture.

It is in no sense to be claimed that studies of scientific value have not been made by those whose primary concern is with the practical applications of anthropology to the problems of European-native contact. Yet it is none the less true that when practical results are the end of such studies, a sense of historical perspective is ordinarily lacking. Whether this is a result of the essentially *ad hoc* approach of research undertaken with practical problems in mind can not be said; to establish the fact, however, no great amount of reading of available publications of this type need be done, nor of the discussions of general problems of policy regarding the directions to be given the changing life of the native.[2]

The concentration on the practical concerns of European-native contact has another consequence that results from this over-specialization on one kind of contact. That from the point of view of culture-history, contacts of the sort now occurring between nationals of colonizing governments and native peoples are of no different order

[1] These points are discussed in Herskovits, (1936).
[2] See, for example, the numerous papers on practical anthropology, its methods and aims, that are found in most recent issues of the journals "Oceania" and "Africa," as well as such works as those of Schrieke (1929), Elkin (1937), Williams (1933), and Westermann (1934).

than those that have certainly occurred since recorded history began
—and perhaps since mankind has inhabited the earth—is something
that seems rarely to hold a place in the underlying approach to the
subject by those concerned with it. An illustration of this may be
taken from one of the most comprehensive studies of culture-contact
that has been carried on from the point of view of practical anthropology: "At no time in the history of mankind has a clash of nations,
peoples, races, and their cultures, traditions, prejudices, interests and
abilities taken place like today."[1] Yet one cannot but wonder whether,
in the light of our historical knowledge of the expansion of the
empires of the Far East as well as of Europe in ancient and medieval
times, to say nothing of the spread of peoples over the non-literate
world, one can speak of a qualitative difference between the contacts of
peoples in earlier times and those that are taking place at present.

There is, furthermore, another consideration that is too often
overlooked by those who are occupied with the problems of applied
anthropology. A basic justification of ethnological research is that
it gives a broad background against which to judge our own rules
of behavior, and a more inclusive view of human cultures than can
be attained by any other social discipline. This is because it alone
offers data against which we can project customs peculiar to ourselves
and, in the manner of scientific research, test generalizations arising
out of the study of the patterns of our culture by seeing whether or
not these generalizations have validity when applied to peoples whose
customs have no historical connection with our own. Are not
anthropologists themselves, in devoting themselves to the study of
the contact between their own culture and native civilizations, likewise
in danger of narrowing, then, the point of view they have attained?
The uncritical tendency to see native cultures everywhere forced out
of existence by the overwhelming drive of European techniques; the
feeling that these "simpler" folk must inevitably accept the sanctions of

[1] Thurnwald (1935), p. 1.

their more efficient rulers as they do some of the outward modes of life of those under whose control they live; all these reflect a type of ethnocentrism that should be absent from the scientific studies of an anthropologist. It is for this reason that, to realize to the utmost the scientific gain to be had from studies of culture contact, those situations where nations of Europe or America were or are today in no way involved should be first sought out for study, since here the student who comes from these countries can in no wise identify himself with the processes he is studying. In this manner scientific objectivity will be enhanced; otherwise in its study of cultures in contact, anthropology must suffer, without check, from the same handicaps under which other social sciences labor in neglecting to look beyond the horizon of our own culture.

II

SOME ACCULTURATION STUDIES REVIEWED

I

The preceding section has sought to indicate the earlier uses of the term "acculturation" and its various and often conflicting meanings. A definition of the word has been offered so that studies of acculturation may be oriented from the point of view of the ends to be sought in them; and to make for results of the greatest usefulness in future research into those problems of cultural dynamics that can be studied through an analysis of the principles that govern human behavior under the varying circumstances of contact between peoples of different cultures.

To document and clarify the concepts that underlie both the definition that has been given and the problems in the field of culture contact that are to be outlined in the section that follows, a series of brief analyses are here undertaken of some of the studies of acculturation that have been made. These studies by no means comprehend all those that might have been considered, and in the bibliography, which itself is far from complete, still other titles will be found. However, most of the full-length portraits of individual cultures that today exhibit the effects of prolonged cultural contact are discussed, while certain reports that deal with investigations of the results of acculturation in the field of religion are also presented to indicate the manner in which effective research into a restricted aspect of a single culture experiencing contact, or even into the adventures of a single institution in such a culture can be prosecuted.

In these compressed analyses, the data are presented with the primary purpose in mind of making available to the student the materials at hand, so that he may be the better guided in his field studies. So different are the situations with which the student of culture contact is called upon to deal, and so varied are the methodological problems presented in what is the essentially pioneer work that must be done at the present time in studying acculturation, that it has been felt necessary not only to consider the history of acculturation and the delimitation of the field, the problems that can be most profitably attacked and the cautions that must be observed in studying them, but also to afford those concerned with research of this type the opportunity to follow for themselves the reports upon which the conclusions that will comprise the final section of this work are in large measure based.

2

At the outset, research that presents all phases of the life of acculturated folk may be reviewed. Here, although the nature of the data in each will be sketched, emphasis will be placed on the implications of these studies for the problems of cultural dynamics and the rôle of the individual in cultural change, and on the evaluation of the hypotheses that have been advanced on the basis of these investigations.

a. Parsons, Elsie Clews, *Mitla, Town of the Souls.*[1]

Two reasons, we are told, actuated this study of the Zapotecan town of Mitla in southern Mexico. Specifically, it was undertaken to obtain comparative data to throw light on possible Spanish or Indian derivations of certain aspects of Pueblo Indian cultures. But

[1] Excerpts from this volume are given with the kind permission of the publishers, the University of Chicago Press.

from a broader point of view it was conceived as one which, when taken together with analyses of other Mexican communities, might lay bare "the patterns in Indian-Spanish assimilation and acculturation" and thus "add to the understanding of these fundamental processes of social change not only in Latin America but in society at large." (p. xii)

The greater part of the book is given over to a well-rounded description of the life of the townspeople. Two departures from customary practice mark the presentation, however; a chapter devoted to the neighboring folk relates the culture of Mitla to that of other communities of the region, while another, which details town gossip, reveals much concerning the place of individuals in the community of which they form a part. The final chapter, which breaks down the institutions already described into their Indian or Spanish sources of provenience and considers the amalgamations of customs which derive from both sources, bears most directly on the study of acculturation.

The difficulties in answering the question "Indian or Spanish?" are amply illustrated by the great number of cultural elements whose possible or known provenience must be sought. These range from minutiae of custom to entire institutions, and from material culture to typical states of mind. One point that is made has special significance: that an institution from one culture, in being taken over by another, may gain a new validating concept drawn from aboriginal patterns. This is to be seen in a comment on the phrasing of certain attitudes held by the natives: "The terms are Spanish, but the evaluation, I think, is characteristically Indian. It is based on a person's conduct, and not on his opinions or on his emotional reactions except as expressed in conduct." (p. 481)

Some traits of the culture stand out as clearly Indian, as, for instance the mode of carrying burdens on the back by means of a tumpline, or the manner of greeting visitors. Other traits are as clearly Spanish, though here the usual manifestation of the introduced trait is its outer form rather than the inner response to that form: tiled roofs, wedding rites, Catholic elements in the religious ceremonialism. But in far more cases than would come under either of the preceding classifications, traits are listed as partially of one cultural derivation and partly another; and still more often, as possibly either one or the other, or both. "The ethnologist must squint backward and reconstruct the past as best he can," we are told, and these results indicate the full reward vouchsafed those who expend the effort needed to do this.

A fundamental problem in the study of "cultural assimilation" is, to employ a phrase of the author, the analysis of the use of "something new in accordance with something old." (p. 21) This particular quotation has to do with the adoption of European words into Zapotecan speech, but it might equally apply to almost any other problem of provenience attacked in the book. It recurs again and again: thus the change brought about in the life of women by an electric mill is expressed in terms of the same acculturizing phenomenon, "New goods, but handled, as far as the division of labor by sex is concerned, in the old way." (p. 31) And the same holds true for religion:

"God, the saints, and the spirits of the dead... form the pantheon of present-day Mitla, as of the Republic at large. Included among the saints are the Virgin and Christ, for there are many Virgins and many Christs. Even a saint whose name does not change but is associated with different sanctuaries becomes a kind of split personality or possessed of quite distinct personalities, like brothers... This concept is consistent with the general feeling that saints are local spirits..." (p. 204)

"There is one place in Mitla where, from a historical point of view, the devil is properly allocated. Over the door of the jail... are scratched outlines of devils.... A warning, presumably, to the criminal! A warning, but of what? There is little or no belief in hell... Even when you want to injure an enemy, you do not pray to the Devil, you visit the three crosses of Calvary, at noon time. It is the saints who do your bidding for evil as well as for good, in this life. The saints, the souls, and God are associated, like the Devil, with this life rather than with a future life; they all bestow, or withhold, practical benefits and goods from day to day, just as did the ancient, pre-Conquest gods." (p. 210)

Other instances of this kind and the detailed analyses of the final chapter bring us to the statement of a problem that is fundamental for all studies of acculturation: "Why have these traits survived, why have other traits which we have reason to suppose were once a part of Zapotecan culture not survived, and why have certain features or aspects of which we think as distinctively Spanish traits not been adopted into the culture?" (p. 511)

This leads to the presentation of a series of propositions put forward as "partial answers" to these "basic queries":

"Traits may be preserved merely because of ignorance of anything different; in other words, certain parts of two contacting cultures may not be in contact at all." (pp. 511–512)

"Intermarriage is a more obvious factor in cultural breakdown or cultural assimilation, whichever way you look at it, particularly when the woman belongs to the dominant culture." (p. 512)

"Ignorance of custom, whatever it is due to, is a great protection to custom." (p. 515)

"... an old custom ... [may survive] ... because it is agreeable to the new one." (p. 515)

"When the ceremonial life of a highly ceremonialized community is suppressed, far more of its general culture goes by the board than in the subjection of a people whose culture is less ritualized and less developed." (p. 519)

Illustrations are given of all these assumptions from the past history of Mitla, and a few of such examples can be cited here. Thus, the first hypothesis is illustrated by reference to practices having to do with the life of women; how Mitla Indian women have practically no opportunity of knowing about the "domestic manners and morals" of the mestiza. And instances from elsewhere are also proffered:

"Up to recent years similar conditions held for the Pueblo Indians in relation to the Mexicans and 'Americans' surrounding them, and were a strong factor in Pueblo conservatism, just as nowadays the employment of Pueblo girls in American households is making for the breakdown of Pueblo culture. We are quite familiar with the effect of house service among American Negroes during slavery—plantation Negroes and house servants were very distinct groups—but we have not applied the observation to other cultural contacts, and in applying the platitude that one half does not know how the other half lives to cultural classes within the same group, I doubt if we are fully aware of its significance." (p. 512)

Or, referring to another of these propositions, it is pointed out that it is because a certain region is ministered to only by a visiting priest —whose knowledge of local custom is slight—that such aboriginal rites as turkey-sacrifice and cave-visiting have survived.

Other mechanisms that have been operative in framing present-day Zapotecan culture are then considered, with particular reference to that mode of accommodation to newly introduced cultural elements termed "change by substitution." "We have been wont to say," it is stated, "that new traits tend to be welcomed or readily borrowed if they do not clash with pre-existent traits, or again if they have something in common with pre-existent traits to take the edge off their unfamiliarity." (p. 521) This is of the order of adaptation which, in the study of religion among New World Negroes, has been termed cultural syncretism; and a striking exemplification of the process in Mitla is given in the following passage:

"Just as the friars and priests built their monastery and curacy and their new churches over the temples, using the ancient stones in new construction, so they got support, when they could, from native culture for their calendar, their ceremonies and ritual, their pantheon and their hagiology. In this they were abetted, of course, by the people themselves. It was a circle of assimilation or acculturation in which it would be impossible in most cases to pick out the respective agents. No doubt it was the padres who had crosses raised at all places known or suspected to be associated with aboriginal cults; or if these places did not lend themselves to this technique it was the padres who bedeviled them.... On the other hand, no doubt, ... calling an *idolo* a *santito* or Lightning the messenger of Dios or Solomon the mason of the temples or thinking of the saints as Mitleyenos who, like the early gods, were turned into stone were purely Indian attempts at assimilation. But these are exceptionally clear cases of agency in the long list of changes by substitution that we think took place in Zapotecan post-Conquest history, substitutions which for the most part, in so far as they knew about them, would have been favored, if not suggested, by the Catholics." (pp. 520–521)

Hence this trick of "giving an old habit of mind a new expression" brought it about that "the new religion was after all not so new," and, by implication, that the new culture was also one that retained much of the old.

Those traits are also considered which have been rejected "in accordance with the obverse of the prime principle of assimilation; i. e., when the new trait is too unfamiliar, offering nothing to tie up to, or is quite incompatable with the old trait, not yielding to any process of identification, it will be rejected." (p. 528) Here come varied aspects of Spanish culture; those dependent on language, certain aspects of sex life, habits of mind and attitudes such as partisanship and assertive leadership, and many of the emotions associated with Catholicism, as well as many of the doctrines of Catholic theology. Failure to take over technological traits is laid to poverty, not to lack of desire; "when the new economic way is cheaper, as, for example, a woman's cotton dress as against the woolen, it is quickly substituted." (p. 532) And the reason held, at least in part, to lie behind the failure to adopt such customs of ceremony as a church wedding, which is costly, is also this economic one.

The methodological emphasis placed at the end of this book on the desirability of correlating ethnological findings in studies of this type not only with the early history of a people but also with the available archaeological materials that bear on their past should be kept in mind for use elsewhere. And a final conclusion in like manner is worthy of being remembered when research in other cultures of hybrid origin offers further opportunities for testing such an hypothesis as to the processes of acculturation as this:

"It would appear that changes in social organization and in material culture are made more readily than changes in personal habits and in emotional attitudes, and that a foreign complex is established in its entirety only when it can be fitted into an old form of behavior and is compatible with existing emotional attitudes." (p. 536)

b. Redfield, Robert, *Tepoztlan, a Mexican Village*.[1]

The rounded picture of life in the central Mexican community described in this book, when viewed in conjunction with the materials in the volume just discussed, gives a lively sense of the resemblances and differences between two related cultures which have both been subjected to similar historical experiences. Here, however, the similarity between the two volumes ends, for while one is an analysis of a Mexican culture in terms of its Indian and Spanish affiliations and has as its purpose the determination of the manner in which the two cultural heritages became merged in present-day institutions and beliefs, the other with which we are concerned here employs a different method to deal with a different problem.

This method is developed at some length in the preface. Its essence is found in a passage which, in the book, follows a discussion wherein the growing interest of ethnologists in problems of cultural dynamics is contrasted with their willingness in the past to rest

---

[1] Excerpts from this volume are given with the kind permission of the publishers, the University of Chicago Press.

content "with the mere description of cultures or the solution of specific historic sequences," The author then continues:

"If the interest of the student lies in an investigation of social processes in general terms, it would seem a more direct procedure to study such processes as they actually occur, rather than to content one's self with comparing the historical sequences so laboriously determined by historical methods of the ethnologist, who works without the direct sources of written matter. In sequences of the latter sort only a small part of all the facts can ever be recaptured. If one is interested in studying what happens rather than what happened, one moves more directly if one studies it as it happens. Now that the power and personnel of anthropology has grown, it can undertake such investigations and still continue its work of preserving the record of dying cultures." (p. 12)

To study the "more isolated groups of Mexico" so as to learn of pre-Columbian cultures and "the changes which they underwent when they came in contact with the Spaniards" is possible and, by implication, worthy of attention; but "such a study would be ... of a dead culture and of a past change" and hence "such was not the interest that took the writer to Mexico." For though "to learn as much as can be learned of the history of the present culture of Tepoztlan is a part of any thorough study of that culture," and hence must be an essential part of any attempt to make an ethnographic analysis of it, the principal emphasis is here laid on current changes rather than those which took place in the past.

The approach that is used is based on the concept of the folk culture, which is held to differ significantly from the culture of sophisticated societies. The difference between the mode of studying cultural change when approached in this manner, and that found in the volume just analyzed, which despite the fact that this work preceded the other by seven years is expressed as clearly as though it had been written with the later work in mind, is set forth as follows:

"The Mexican folk are not necessarily Indian. The folk culture is a fusion of Indian and Spanish elements. The acculturation which gave rise to this mixed culture took place three hundred years ago, largely within the first few generations after the Conquest. The analysis of the Mexican folk culture into Spanish and Indian elements is one problem—a historical problem. The description of changes occurring in that folk culture due to spread of city ways is another problem—a study of contemporary change. The disorganization and perhaps the reorganization of the culture here considered under the slowly growing influence of the city is a process—a diffusion process—which can and will be studied. It is, the writer assumes, an example, within convenient limits, of the general type of change whereby primitive man becomes civilized man, the rustic becomes the urbanite." (pp. 13–14)

As is shown in the first chapter, where the location of the village in relation to its surroundings is given, the study essentially resolves itself into an analysis of cultural change in another of those possible situations where control can be exerted over the data. This is apparent from the way in which the ethnic composition of the great plateau of central Mexico, wherein Tepoztlan is situated, is summarized:

"These aboriginal remnants [that inhabit the periphery] and the sophisticated minority in the capital represent the two extremes of Mexican culture: the one urban in character and European in origin, the other Indian and tribal. But the vast middle ground is occupied by people whose culture is neither tribal nor cosmopolitan. Their simple rural way of life is the product of ancient fusion between Indian and Spanish custom." (p. 16)

The approach, therefore, centers on studying the present-day life of the Tepoztecos as this reflects a mingling of the cultures found at the center and at the periphery of the area in which it occupies a minute portion. And as the question inevitably comes to mind, whether this is not really the problem attacked by Parsons translated into distributional terms on a single time level, the answer, a partial, though not completely affirmative one, is afforded us in the descriptions of the life of the village and of the various classes of its inhabitants.

In the actual presentation of data, the procedure followed is like that in other acculturation studies, and there is ample reference of traits to their sources. The opening sentence of the descriptive section reads: "The material culture of Tepoztlan, in contrast to the non-material culture, preserves unmodified a large number of pre-Columbian traits" (p. 31), and the tabulation at the end of the first chapter which gives the Spanish, Indian or mixed sources of origin of the elements in material culture is perhaps one of the most elaborate attempts at referring traits of a mixed culture to specific sources of historical origin to be found in the literature of culture contact. In treating non-material aspects of the culture, where the carry-over of Indian customs is least apparent, the same approach is present, as is to be seen in the description of the marriage ceremony, which is prefaced with the statement that the ritual "has, in general, a simple Catholic form. Most of the features of the old Aztec customs ... have been displaced by Christian-church ritual. But certain elements remain ...." (p. 140) Similarly in discussing magical and medical practices, reference is made to points of derivation.

In the concluding chapters, where the difference between the analysis of Tepoztlan culture and other studies of this type is emphasized, the effect of contact with the city, and the consequences of literacy among a certain section of the population, are first discussed. In accordance with the methodological point of view of the book, the present types of written folk-literature are reproduced rather than the earlier oral types:

"If the purpose of the present study had been to rescue disappearing elements of a more primitive culture, it would have been indicated to collect materials of this sort. But these older, traditional folk tales do not constitute the songs and stories of meaning and significance to the Tepoztecos. A few people tell these stories, usually to children... This body of folk lore is passing through the nursery to oblivion. It is no longer vital; it does not enter into the important social situations in Tepoztlan." (p. 173)

Hence the figures of the revolutionary heroes of recent Mexico rather than the mythical characters of an earlier mythology move through the succeeding pages; printed ballads rather than traditional songs are reproduced.

The final chapter points the data of the preceding pages to establish their appropriateness to the theoretical assumptions. Again, we are told that "the culture of Tepoztlan appears to represent a type intermediate between the primitive tribe and the modern city"; that "only from the point of view of history or of romantic appreciation is Tepoztlan an 'Aztec pueblo'." (pp. 217-218) And the advantages that are held to accrue from the study of a community of this kind in terms of the gain in understanding cultural dynamics is again pointed out, though this time from a somewhat different point of view:

"...if the interest is not in depiction, but in studying social change as it takes place... then Tepoztlan presents an excellent opportunity. This opportunity is for the study of the change whereby a folk community is slowly becoming more like the city. This change is a case of diffusion, occurring in an easily observed situation, so slowly as not to accomplish the disorganization of the community, and under practical circumstances which liberate the student from responsibility to record the fragmentary vestiges of a disappearing culture." (p. 218)

And because not only the diffusion of "the traits usually listed, of technique and ritual" can be studied effectively in this manner, but also "what can ... be called 'subjective' traits: mental form as well as mental content," it is further concluded that this kind of situation is one in which research into the inner psychology, as well as outer forms, of the "culture process" must yield rich results.

That this approach represents the kind of control sought in all acculturation studies is evident, and to the degree that studies of peoples undergoing acculturation are made in the effort to understand the workings of cultural change, there is practical identity in the ends that are sought. The situation studied in Tepoztlan may well be studied elsewhere than in Mexico, but such investigations only differ from studies of acculturation in the matter of the emphasis placed on the time element. For it is evident that the culture of the "folk" and of urban sophisticates must be of an order of difference that is quite the same as that which obtains between peoples of different historical background whose contacts have resulted in cultural interchange. That this is recognized to be the case is apparent from the following comment which, but for one sentence, concludes the book:

"They are changes which have resulted... out of the conflict between the two cultures in which, mentally, [the Tepoztecan] is living at the same time." (p. 223)

c. Mead, Margaret, *The Changing Culture of an Indian Tribe.*

With this study of the contemporary life of a North American tribe, we come to the type of acculturative situation in which research is most currently being carried on—where contact in recent historic times has occurred between whites and native folk. The methodological problems faced by the author here offer less difficulties than those which must be dealt with in studying Mexican groups where the initial impulses of contact set in long ago. Here the contact has been so recent that an adjustment of the kind reached by the people described in the two volumes just discussed has not been possible to achieve, and the disorganization resulting from recent or continuing contact is a prime factor.

The mode of presentation in this book is the one mandatory in any description of a people undergoing, or who have undergone, acculturation—the cultural base, the impinging forces, and the resulting change in the receiving group. It is possible, too, here to pay some attention to the attitudes of the donor group, and use is made of the much more satisfactory historical data that are to be had regarding the nature of the contacts. The nexus of the volume—the data concerning the life of the people—is laid between an initial statement of approach, and a final consideration of the place of women in the culture as it exists today, especially as this throws light on the maladjustment of the folk at the present time.

"The Antlers," as the anonymous tribe who are the subject of the book are designated, are the remnants of a Plains Indian people who led a semi-hunting, semi-agricultural existence. With their social organization based on a gentile system, religion marked by the vision quest, sacred bundles, and secret societies for war and healing in which women played a minor rôle, they lived the usual well-adjusted life of any undisturbed tribe. Three periods of adjustment followed their initial unimportant contacts with whites. The first was during the days of the fur trade, when with the introduction of guns and steel traps the dislocation of aboriginal economic life commenced. The second is marked by the coming of white settlers to the region, the establishment of an Indian agency and a Presbyterian mission, and the disappearance of the buffalo. In the third period—"under double pressure—from government and missionary on the one hand, and from forward-looking optimistic leaders on the other—the people abandoned earth lodges, tipis, hunting, trapping, and fishing, and settled down in the last quarter of the nineteenth century to an existence which had a superficial resemblance to a rural American community." (p. 24)

Thus, at the turn of the century, "the Antlers might be said to have made a second adjustment to white culture ... They had made for themselves a sort of existence, although it was only a shadow of the rich complexity of their former lives. It was, however, a coherent standard, which, had its economic basis been left undisturbed, might have successfully defied further modification for a generation, or perhaps more." (pp. 29–30) But this was not to be. Because after a period of twenty-five years that had ill equipped the Indian to cope with the new situation with which he was presented, there was an "onrush of white settlement, coincident with the 'period of trust' when by act of Congress the Indians were to receive fee patents to their lands." (p. 30) And since this broke down the last protective barrier which might have been reared about these Indians, they found themselves at the mercy of the dominant group among whom they were henceforth to live.

The closeness of the whites and Indians on the reservation as it was constituted in 1932, the time of the writing of this book, is stressed; though it must be noted that some of these observations may be invalid because of the present policy of the Indian Bureau, especially with regard to allotted land. "Everywhere Indian land abuts on white-owned land .... (p. 34) The reservation and the reservation towns present this external picture of a mixed population, using the same roads, driving in the same kind of vehicles, trading at the same stores ..." (p. 37) and in many other ways leading the same kind of life. Yet this apparent mingling is not an actual one. "The distribution of whites and Indians over the same territory does not make for much contact between the races" (p.36), for the psychology of both groups lays emphasis on group distinctions: "This continual contact in a familiar setting only seems to strengthen the popular white belief that the Indians are merely bad and inefficient editions of themselves, and encourages them to set down the deficiency of the Indian to his race, not to his culture." (p. 37)

The acculturative forces are hence those of governmental pressure, and, in a negative sense, the refusal of the whites to permit the Indians to enter into the life of the community, except where advances are made to an individual Indian who has something of value that can be acquired to advantage by a white neighbor, or where political matters are involved, since the Indians of this particular tribe have the vote. Against this background the economic, political, social, religous, and educational situations of the Indians are projected, to be considered in terms of the deviations from aboriginal custom shown by their contemporary form, and the psychological effect of the resulting cultural disequilibrium.

In all these aspects of culture, save only the religious, much the same tale of cultural chaos is told. If the economic life be taken as an example, we see how, on the basis of a concept of wealth as a means to validate position by the accumulation of "merit ratings through the public distribution" of one's belongings, of a system which admitted no inheritance of property, of land as something that approached a free good except when in actual use, these people have been projected into a system where private property, both in goods and land, is paramount, and where to give wealth away means to deprive oneself and one's family of the very necessities of life. Yet the economic ideas of the Indian's past "are actually the economic ideas which be retains today. For the situations which have resulted from white contact he has a separate ideology. His actual personal property is sometimes expended according to one set of ideas and sometimes to the other." (p. 45) The old patterns of the "give away" exist in attenuated form, while the "compulsion to provide for anyone who enters one's house," something regulated in aboriginal times by the functioning organization of the society, has lost its checks and balances with disastrous results. It is retained only in small matters, but an "extreme selfishness" rules where the great sums that uncomprehended circumstances sometimes thrust on the unprepared Indian are disposed of with the profligacy that is encouraged by those whites who are not slow to grasp the opportunities thus afforded them.

The course of "Antler" religious life seems to have been one of disintegration and then, through the coming of the Peyote cult, of subsequent reintegration. With the advent of Presbyterian missionaries the aboriginal beliefs and rites all but disappeared, so that at the end of the first period of adjustment, all the Indians were at least nominal Presbyterians. Yet the desultory Presbyterian ritual gave little satisfaction, so that when the Peyote cult was introduced, its incorporation of certain tenets of Christianity into the aboriginal patterns of ceremonialism found the people ripe to adopt it. Today the Peyote cult continues as the prevailing religion, and though its rites no longer engross the people, it continues to hold their allegiance. Of aboriginal religion, only the beliefs and attitudes toward the dead, and the fear of the supernatural punishment termed *nonka* that follows on disrespect of the old ceremonial objects that have not been sold or lost, continue.

The system of governmental education was responsible for much of the breaking down of earlier mores. As described in this book, since it presents a picture of conditions under an Indian policy no longer in effect, it is of interest to the student concerned with acculturation principally as an historical statement. This is especially true of the account of the "outing" system of still earlier days, whereby those who were sent east to school spent the summers working in the homes of Quaker farmers, where they were treated quite as members of the family. Included in this discussion of education, however, is a highly significant passage which hints at acculturation in linguistic usage, and is of great value as a lead for further research into the facts concerning the results of acculturation in the field of speech.

With this sketch of the results of culture-contact among the "Antlers," the place of this report among acculturation studies may be considered in other respects than those already discussed. Essentially a study in social demoralization, the presentation is understandably marked by the distress of a sympathetic observer at the unfortunate conditions under which these Indians have come to live. The question for the student of cultural contact is, however, whether these conditions of life are not sufficiently exceptional so as to make them pathological even among the cases of brutal contact between natives and whites known to us from other parts of the world. From a methodological point of view, the situation would thus seem to be so extreme that, at this stage of the study of culture contact, the aid it can give to an understanding of the dynamics of cultural change must be materially less than that afforded by research among a tribe where penalty for being in the path of white expansion has been less drastic.

The great emphasis placed in this study on the impact of white culture on the "Antlers," furthermore, tends to obscure the effect on the same people of a highly significant process of inter-tribal acculturation that the book implies is going on among the Indians themselves. It would undoubtedly have been very illuminating if the fact that the "Antler" takes refuge from his sense of a loss of tribal dignity through identifying himself with the larger group, "the American Indian," had been further probed. For it would seem that the fact that he is today thrown into much closer contact than ever before with other "American Indians" who, like himself, have embraced this new affiliation, must be of the greatest importance in obtaining the picture both of his outer and inner life that is the aim of this study.

The theoretical discussion of acculturation differentiates the practical from the scientific study of cultures in contact in the manner referred to in the preceding section;[1] it states the difficulties in the way of studying changing cultures as against the problems in the description of life in "stable" communities; and indicates the contributions the study of changing societies of this type may be expected

[1] See above, p. 5.

to make to our knowledge of the processes of cultural change. It is the author's conviction that, to the historian, research into the lives of peoples undergoing culture-contact will "show sufficiently general tendencies so that any detailed study of one group at one time will be ... data upon much wider historical events" (p. 8), while for those concerned with cultural dynamics, the "study of human societies in peculiar conditions of disequilibrium ... should serve to illuminate the social process, to give the type of understanding which springs from the very characteristic which makes it in other respects so unsatisfactory—distortion." (p. 15)

The effect of the present conditions of tribal life upon the "Antler" woman, and the way this is reflected in the behavior of all the members of the tribe constitutes the final portion of this work. The oft repeated statement concerning the conservatism of women as against that of men is in this discussion formulated as a general principle. Yet the "Antler" woman, in the sphere of religion, for example, or in the economic aspects of her life, is not shown to have changed her behavior to a strikingly lesser degree than have the men of her tribe. The statement of principle regarding differences in sex receptivity to the new thus may stand as one to be further tested, for though among the "Antlers" the verdict is "not proven," the contention is lodged deeply enough in anthropological assumption to merit its careful investigation.

One point suggested in the preceding chapter may be recalled here as especially pertinent to a discussion of the approach to the data inherent in this work. This has to do with the retention of historical perspective by the student who deals with a tribe such as this, where the clinical picture dictates a diagnosis of extreme demoralization. To recognize this fact does not necessarily impel one either to draw the conclusion that demoralization is inevitable when native folk come in contact with European cultures, or that contact of this kind must lead to tribal doom. As a matter of recorded fact, it is known that throughout history, though stronger peoples have imposed their wills on weaker ones, these have made their adjustments, completed their acculturation, and survived to carry on their lives and much of their earlier tradition. And though it may yet be demonstrated that "the process of cultural disintegration in which the inevitable progress of the more complex culture gradually breaks down the native culture is as meaningless, as random, as is the collapse of a house before a wrecking machine," yet our very attempts to discern principles of cultural dynamics in our study of the contacts of peoples would seem in itself to constitute a denial of this principle. It is likewise to be questioned whether the individual who is "left floundering in a heterogeneous welter of meaningless uncoordinated and disintegrating institutions" must develop the "formless uncoordinated character" that is ascribed to him. The "Antlers," we are told, were themselves in a fair way to making a reasonably satisfactory adjustment to their new conditions of life at the end of the past century. The Indians of Mexico have made such an adjustment, and so have the Negroes of the New World, though they were subjected to far more rigorous treatment and to an all-embracing detribalization such as the "Antlers" were never called upon to face. It is thus not too much to suggest, as we attempt to rescue our sense of historic perspective from the assaults made upon it by our emotions when we regard the actual condition of a primitive group such as this, that the "Antlers" may in the future make an adjustment to their present conditions of life comparable to that which they had already once made.

The mode of presentation of data in this work also merits consideration as a procedural problem. Students of cultural contact, especially those who study native-white contact, are often confronted with a difficult decision when preparing their field materials for publication, since this must often be done so as to obviate any possible embarrassment or, in some cases, actual inconvenience to those who have given them information. That a certain measure of concealment is absolutely necessary—to a degree unknown when "undisturbed" primitive cultures are described—must be recognized. But the extent to which concealment can be achieved and still not vitiate the scientific usefulness of the resulting work is a matter of the utmost importance. This study represents the most extreme degree of concealment; not only are individuals given names other than their own and the tribal name itself changed, but the names of neighboring Indian tribes are also disguised, the reservation is not designated, and even the state where the Indians live is deleted. Yet references are made to earlier literature concerning this people (pp. 91, for instance, or 202–203) which, lacking any clues, the reader who wishes to go to these sources is at the mercy of casual word-of-mouth information concerning the tribal name, and the common procedure of checking scientific data is made a matter of chance. No solution of this practical difficulty can be suggested, unless it be agreed for the present that, since the field is so wide, only those situations should be studied where at least tribal names and the locale of the work can be revealed. For it is evident that where such elaborate concealment is attempted in a work as useful as this, much of its value to students concerned with the same problems must inevitably be lost.

d. Radin, Paul, *The Influence of the Whites on Winnebago Culture.*

As an essential preliminary to setting forth the problems considered in this paper, the background of present-day Winnebago customs and beliefs is first presented in terms of their early history and aboriginal life. The author then proceeds on this basis to outline the results of the contact between the Winnebago and the whites in the following terms:

"The influence of European cultures has taken four definite lines; it has either completely obliterated Winnebago customs; it has in-

troduced ideas, customs, and utensils of European origin; it has
brought into contact with one another Indian tribes that had had
little or no intercourse before; or, finally, it has stimulated contact
already existing before the coming of the white man." (p. 142)

The first of these consequences, it is pointed out, did not necessarily
result from the pursuit of a definite policy; it is rather that the
encroachment of the whites on Indian territory and the movement
of the frontier "made impossible a number of Indian activities, and
brought about situations new to Winnebago history." The breakdown
of the clan system is thus to be thought of as having resulted from the
"ceaseless shifting of position from one place to another...and the
intermarriage with whites or Indians of other tribes, [which] played
havoc with an individual's status." Likewise, the manner in which
the individualities of small village groups were suppressed by being
drawn together into a single unit is held to be the result of the
operation of the same impersonal historic circumstance. "When they
were all forced together, there was an intermingling such as had not
been known before, with the result that some things disappeared,
while others were unduly emphasized." (pp. 142–143) Further
examples are the predominance of the Thunder-Bird and Bear clans,
which, owing to their larger membership, were enabled to assert
greater supremacy when the Winnebago were concentrated than
would have been possible under their scattered distribution before white contact; and the diffusion of the Medicine Dance
which, introduced through the Sauk, spread much more rapidly
among the Winnebago than could have been possible in aboriginal
times.

Aside from material objects, only three concepts, all in the field of
religion, can be traced to white culture, and all have a substantial
basis in aboriginal Winnebago belief. These are "the concept of
Earth-maker; the concept of the chief of the bad spirits; and the
cross symbol associated with Earth-maker." (p. 143)

"However, what approaches to the Christian concept of God in Earth-maker is found principally in the origin myths of the various ceremonies, and can be adequately explained as a result of shamanistic systematization of beliefs. The concept of the Great Evil Spirit is, as I have suggested, merely a variation of the popular Evil Spirit, although it must be admitted that there was a number of Christian traits in the characterization of this figure in the popular Hero cycle of the Twins. The cross is the common symbol of the four cardinal points and of the four winds and has nothing to do with the Christian cross. Its association with Earth-maker is probably accidental. It might still, however, be contended that though all the foregoing beliefs are of unquestionable Winnebago origin, the elaborate origin myth in the Medicine Dance does suggest a stimulation on the part of Christian beliefs. To this no answer can be given, except that it is possible." (pp. 143–144)

In the realm of material culture, however, the traits introduced by the whites were legion; while "the introduction of the white man's tools . . . produced a veritable revolution in Winnebago manufacture." They were taken up at once, and so effectively that the memory of pre-white techniques is almost lost. As might be expected, this was because of their greater efficiency, which, for example, permitted the more durable dugout to replace the birch-bark canoe:

"The introduction of European utensils possesses a peculiar interest, for, with the exception of ornamentation, it is the only subject of Indian life that can be discussed historically, from the point of view of the Indian mind and old Indian utensils upon borrowed elements. No such studies have as yet been made, but when they shall have been it will, I am certain, become patent that the process of borrowing was not a passive one; that wherever possible the new utensils soon became assimilated to old Indian forms; and that even with regard to such novel articles as the saddle and the whip, Indian methods of manufacture exercised a due amount of influence." (pp. 144–145)

As far as is known, this study, suggested in 1913, is still to be made —either among the Winnebago or any other Indian tribe, or, indeed, elsewhere in the world. It not only involves a detailed analysis of the elements of European and native culture (granting that no two native cultures in contact are well enough known to permit of this procedure) but also a thorough consideration of the setting of these material objects in the new cultural amalgam. In the field of religion a few studies cast along these lines have been undertaken, notably of the Ghost Dance and the Hand Game associated with it, but this particular research, suggested two decades ago, still lies in the future.

The final two points concerning the results of contact with European culture, which present the greatest methodological difficulties, are treated as a series of stimulating questions, which can best be indicated in the words of their author:

"... What was the role of the white trader in bringing into closer contact with the Winnebago, both their Algonkin neighbors and more distant tribes? This question is of transcendent importance because it may have an all-important bearing on the sameness in material culture, religious beliefs, and, to a large extent, mythology, of the culture area known as the Woodland. This particular factor in the development of uniformity in a culture area has never been investigated. It deserves, however, the most careful attention, for there can be no doubt that through the influence of the white trader there was a closer drawing together of Indian tribes, a greater percentage of intermarriage, and a greater and more systematic interchange of goods and ideas. It is tantalizing that no details are available or likely to be available. For this reason we must seize upon all the bits of evidence we can obtain; if the Winnebago tell us that previous to the coming of the whites little of any woodenware was used, and if, not long after, we find in common use among the Winnebago, woodenware indistinguishable from that of their Algonkin neighbors, the most plausible inference is that it was the Algonkin woodenware, and that its rapid dissemination followed in the trail of the white trader." (p. 145)

This point must be underscored as one that has been almost completely overlooked in studies of culture-contact, and will be considered in the next section of this discussion. It is interesting that this opportunity has not been utilized for, once set forth, it is evident that persons such as traders who circulate freely from one tribe to another must be important agents of diffusion and, whether or not an actual factor in acculturation, must certainly prepare the way for acculturation when prolonged contact does take place. That the operation of this particular mechanism in the exact way suggested can no longer be studied among the Indians of the United States would seem to be the case; in Africa, however, where not only whites, but, in East Africa the British Indians and Arabs constitute an acculturative force of this kind, and, in West Africa, where the Hausa traders take objects over all the vast stretch of the Guinea Coast and inland toward the western Sudan, it should be susceptible of investigation. Similarly, in the Far East, Chinese traders are today playing the same rôle among the native peoples of the Philippines, let us say, as did the white traders among the Indians. And since the aspects of material culture carried from one people to another by such means are the most easily discernible of all traits, this problem is one which, not only because of its promise, but because of its methodological practicability, deserves attention on the part of students.

e. Herskovits, Melville J., *Life in a Haitian Valley*.

The approach to acculturation in this volume is essentially that developed in the preceding section of this discussion, and hence it is unnecessary to comment on those parts where theoretical problems are discussed. It will suffice here to point out the peculiarities in the situation studied, and the manner in which these affected the methodological approach.

In a way, the problems of procedure presented in studying the life of the Haitian peasant exhibit resemblances both to those that confront students who consider Mexican culture in terms of its past contacts and present forms, and to those who analyze the processes of acculturation elsewhere among peoples such as the American Indians, or South or East Africans, where the contact of native peoples with whites is going on at the present time. For, like the Mexican, the contact with European culture experienced by the Africans who were brought to the island of Haiti as slaves ceased many years ago, and what remains is the result of acculturation as it has worked itself out after a considerable period of time, during which there has been a minimum of disturbance from the outside. On the other hand, the Haitian situation resembles those in the second category in that, though it is something of the past rather than the present, the excellent historical documents make it possible to recover the circumstances of acculturation to a degree of detail not much less than in the case of these more recent contacts.

Since the culture of Haiti is a derivative of West African and French patterns, it was first of all necessary to discover the tribes from which the Negroes had been drawn, and what social and economic strata in the African population these represented; it was equally important to determine what types the French contributed to the population of the island during the period that Haiti was a colony of France. And, having done this, it was possible to describe the outlines of the West African civilizations from which the preponderant cultural importations were made, and the mode of life of the French masters, which in turn provided an understanding of the background out of which the present-day culture has grown. This background was then drawn on to assess the provenience of specific aspects of culture, and of attitudes and modes of behavior of the people, as they exist today.

Actually, the method to be followed in attacking these questions of provenience is a dual one, in which the reciprocal relationship of history to ethnology is clearly to be seen. In this case, for example, it is only in the documents that the necessary accounts of the customs, and names of places, persons and deities of West Africa that are essential if we are to establish tribal sources of origin can be found. On the other hand, without knowing the ethnology of West Africa, many promising leads in these same documents would pass unrecognized, since even such important hints as tribal names would be, as they actually have been, disregarded by one lacking knowledge of the tribal distributions of West Africa. The ethnologist who studies the customs of the Haitians has also another tool to use in determining cultural origins. Knowledge of the names of gods in the present-day "voodoo" cult, or a grasp on those other aspects of Haitian culture which take specific West African form, such as the cooperative societies, can also aid in determining identifications of the contributing cultures.

With an understanding of the historical background from which Haitian culture derived, the present-day manifestations of this culture as found in a single valley of the island are first described, and then analyzed in terms of the manner in which they have developed out of their acculturative background. As always, any attempt of this kind must be based on the outer patterns of the culture—or, if a different and more customary phrasing be employed, must be concerned with tracing the traits of the culture to their sources. As has been remarked in the preceding section, however, this is not enough, and therefore not only "traits" are presented in their objective manifestations, but attitudes, points of view, and those psychological mechanisms which underlie these outer forms are considered as well. In addition, the syncretism of the contributing cultures, especially in the field of religion, is analyzed, since here, as in all other cultures that are undergoing or have undergone continuous contact with civilizations different than themselves, not only have aspects of the two sets of traditions diplaced each other in far from equal degree, but similar phases of the two cultures party to the contact have tended to form customs that are relatively new.

This study, then, seeks to establish the origin of as many elements of the culture studied as possible, but in its descriptive approach presents the culture as it exists here and now as a living entity. The problem of the manner in which the Negroes of different tribes integrated their varied civilizations in the face of exposure to French culture is also studied when such matters as the derivation of deities of the "voodoo" cult are considered. A future line of investigation into the manner in which a situation of cultural mixture such as is found in Haiti reacts on the personalities of its carriers is also indicated in the concept of "socialized ambivalence," which is advanced to explain the emotional instability of the Haitian peasant that has arisen out of the stresses resultant on the conflicts in his dual cultural heritage.

f. Schapera, I., *The Contributions of Western Civilization to Modern Kxatla Culture.*

As part of a long-time research program dealing with the effect of European contact on this South African tribe, the contribution to be considered here must be regarded as but one of a number of related papers published by the author. Reference has been made in the first section of this book[1] to another of these papers where field techniques employed in studying the BaKxatla are analyzed and methodological principles are indicated which, though made use of in this particular investigation, can also be used in studying other peoples who live under conditions of culture contact.

Recapitulated, these methodological steps are to obtain "as full an account as possible of the existing tribal culture" (which involves, it will be remembered, as full an account of the European modes of behavior that are present as of the more exotic aboriginal traditions); to reconstruct tribal culture as it existed prior to the contact; to

[1] See above, pp. 18-19.

recover as much of the circumstances of the contact as is possible from historical documents and the testimony of those, both native and European, who can draw on actual experience; and finally, to synthesize this material and point it toward explaining the changes which have actually occurred, or toward accounting for resistance to those aspects of the foreign culture which, though presented to the natives, have never been hospitably received by the tribe.

This method is well illustrated by the author's treatment of his data in the present paper. After an outline of the aboriginal culture of the tribe, the types of contact which it has undergone are reviewed. These are found to have been both direct and indirect—these people, on Reserve, have since their first experience with the whites been more or less constantly in direct touch with traders, missionaries, and government officials; but an equally important source of the transmission of European culture has been through the system by which men go from the Reserve to work "in the urban and rural areas of the Transvaal and other European settlements," where they "come into contact with Western civilization in its most developed South African form" and "also encounter representatives of many other native tribes."

The historical approach is fully utilized in the author's consideration of the manner and order of presentation of European culture to these folk. European elements, it is seen, did by no means all appear simultaneously, just as the aims behind their presentation were not at all the same in the case of the various agencies through which they reached the Kxatla:

"The aim of the Mission...seeks essentially to convert the heathen native to Christianity. In pursuit of this policy it seeks also to introduce a new system of morals and general behaviour conforming to Christian ideals, and... further undertakes the secondary task of promoting the general social and material advancement of the people. The Administration is concerned primarily with the maintenance of law and order, and with meeting the cost of the necessary machinery. Such services as education and economic development were not seriously taken in hand until much later. The trader, in so far as he has any definable aim at all, is there to exploit the natives for his own economic benefit, and accordingly attempts to develop as good a market as he can for his wares." (p. 225)

The attitudes toward native life held by each of these agencies, and the methods they employed to achieve their aims, were quite different; and this difference must have had a discernible effect:

"As a result of these contacts, certain traits of culture formerly possessed by the BaKxatla have either disappeared completely or appear to be doing so, others have been much or only slightly modified, and still others appear to have remained largely intact. Other traits, again, have been taken over wholly or in part from Western civilization. Some have been widely accepted, others only to a limited extent." (p. 227)

The questions "Why have some of these changes taken place, and why have they varied so much in their nature and effect?" naturally follow, and the answers, in accordance with their significance for the study of cultural change, occupy the principal portion of the remainder of the paper.

The initial acceptance of various traits of European culture and the secondary developments that resulted from this acceptance are illustrated with numerous examples. The degree to which acceptance was optional with the natives—as in the case of the wares of the traders—or forced upon them—as with certain administrative measures, such as taxation—is discussed, and here the influence of individual personalities is considered. For instance, it is on historic record that the baptism of a chief (Lentswe, who ruled from 1875 to 1921), was the determining factor in bringing about the acceptance of Christianity by the body of the people, while this same tribal head and his successor were primary instruments in causing the adoption of many other phases of European culture. The secondary results of the introduction of these new elements were of equal if not greater importance:

"The acceptance of these culture traits from the Europeans led in time to the disappearance or modification of existing institutions, and to the introduction or development of other new forms of culture." (p. 230)

Some of these were: the rise of new occupations at home; the extension of the activities of the chief; an increase in tribal legislation to cope with new conditions; an increasing demand for trade goods; the establishment of Sunday as a day of rest; a spreading knowledge of the English language.

As may be imagined, the acceptance of European traits has not been uniform:

"Some people are very conservative, while others have discarded many of the traditional customs and beliefs in favour of European institutions. The distribution of European traits varies from an almost universal acceptance of clothing and certain other material objects to an almost negligible adoption of European standards of life and conduct in general." (p. 233)

Some of the internal groupings within the tribe which accepted the proffered traits to different degrees are specified. Those who have had European education do not react in the same manner as those who have not had it. Another dividing line is that of sex—"The men have on the whole been more exposed to European influences, mainly as a result of labour migration . . . But in one respect the women have taken to Western civilization far more extensively than the men. The great majority of Church members are women . . ." (p. 234) Wealth is a factor, and so is the one of European religious affiliation—and differences are likewise to be seen between Church members and "what may best be described as 'nonconformists'."

The problem of resistance to European patterns and traits is also considered. Thus, though there has been a "wide-spread and rapid adoption of European material products, relatively slight progress has been made in subsistence activities." The explanation for this is to be found in the earlier economy of the Kxatla, which was the typical East African one of cattle-raising and the production of crops for subsistence. "Slowness in change ... in political and social organization" is also to be discerned, and this is attributed to "the absence of much direct attack upon their solidarity," though a decreasing incidence of polygyny is to be excepted from this statement. Curious contrasts in acceptance and rejection are found: "The greatest failure of the Church, and of Western civilization generally has been in regard to magic and sorcery," but "it is difficult to account for the persistence of these beliefs and practices in contrast with the almost complete disappearance of ancestor-worship." (pp. 239–240)

Concerning one point this entire study has particular importance, for it furnishes a case with which to put to the test the assertion encountered all too frequently that the contact of native with European culture has as its inevitable result the destruction of the "weaker" civilization. As we have seen, this is based partially on an absence of perspective that is reinforced by arguments drawn from the present status of some of the Indian tribes of the United States, or of the inhabitants of the Polynesian and certain Melanesian Islands where there is not only cultural degradation but actual depopulation. It is too easily overlooked that some peoples are made of sterner stuff, but Negroes seem to be of this type—whether in Africa, it it may be remarked, or in the New World. Thus despite the impressive length of time since contact has been effected between the BaKxatla and European culture—a contact that has been anything but superficial and has continued now for almost a century—much of aboriginal culture remains, and what has given way has been replaced by foreign traits with but little of that destructive effect that is held inescapably to follow. Indeed, the BaKxatla constitute evidence which those who are impressed with the toughness of native cultures in the face of the vicissitudes of contact with Europeans may well offer in support of their position. The proof that the process among the Kxatla has been one of adjustment rather than disintegration is best seen in the sections dealing with the modifications that both indigenous and introduced traits have undergone. The introduction of the plough, for instance, has led to a series of substitutions for aboriginal custom that have had no perceptibly harmful effect on the native economy, and this result is paralleled in other aspects of present-day tribal life. Borrowed traits, moreover, have been changed in accordance with Kxatla patterns, as, for example, in the case of the Church wedding, which "has been grafted on the old marriage ceremonies, and now forms the first stage, followed by the traditional festivities at the homes of both parties."

The BaKxatla, it is concluded, have "on the whole adapted themselves with considerable success to the impact of Western civilization.... The culture at the present time is not the traditional Bantu culture of the Tswana tribes, nor is it the civilization of the European inhabitants of South Africa. It includes elements of both; but they have been combined into a new and distinctive pattern." (p. 250) This statement is perhaps the most significant conclusion of the entire paper. For it is possible that we have here in actual operation the processes that brought about an amalgam of culture such as can be seen in Mexico and Haiti and other parts of the world, where peoples who were once in continued contact with foreign bodies of tradition have made an adjustment in terms of adaptation to the fashions of living newly introduced. Perhaps this, to a far greater extent than is realized, is the result of most extended contacts between cultures, rather than the more conventionally accepted dictum that contact eventuates in the extinction of one by the other.

g. Hunter, Monica, *Reaction to Conquest, Effects of Contact with
Europeans on the Pondo of South Africa.*

Prefaced with brief references to the historical background of
Pondo contact with Europeans, the nature of this contact, and the
method employed in studying its consequences, this work then
turns to the ethnography of the people who are its principal subjects,
indicating those points at which aboriginal traditions have been
influenced, changed, or replaced by what has been imposed upon
the people by Europeans or willingly taken over from them. The
Bantu folk of South Africa, however, as has been seen in discussing
the work just considered, are not only influenced by whites while they
are on the Reserve, but also when they go away from home to work.
Hence the concluding portions of this book are devoted to descriptions
of their life in one of these urban communities, and on European
farms.

The approach to the subject-matter given in the Introduction is
one that has been commented on in the first chapter of the present
work:

"This book deals with one aspect of this culture contact—the
effect of contact with Europeans upon a Bantu community... To
gauge this change it would be satisfactory to study the society as it
was before it came under these influences, to study the nature of the
influences, and then to observe how it differs from the old culture.
But unfortunately for the student of culture contact, the science of
social anthropology has been developed since the opening up of Africa,
and in the areas to which Europeans came there are no adequate
data on Bantu life as it was before contact with Europeans." (p. 1)

What constitutes "adequate data" is not something on which all
will agree, but it seems strange that it should in South Africa be
necessary to complain of difficulties in recovering enough of aboriginal
modes of life to provide a satisfactory base against which to assess

a measure of cultural change. Happily, neither this methodological intransigeance nor the ethnocentrism implied in the statement seem really to have affected the field work as it was done, for the theoretical position of the author is not only negated by the actual materials that are presented in that part of the book where Pondo life is described, but explicit statements such as that in the paragraph succeeding the one containing the passage quoted show that the approach to the problem was the usual one employed in situations of this kind:

"Among the Pondo, in the reserve community studied, those still living can tell a great deal about life before European influence was strong, and so, besides comparing areas subject to different contact influences we observe change within the one community by comparing accounts of ancients with present conditions, conservative with less conservative families."

This approach is made still more explicit in a later passage:

"My object is firstly to describe life as it is in Pondoland today; but the past determines the present, and in a society which is changing rapidly it is impossible to explain the working of existing institutions without constant reference to the past. Furthermore, data given by ancients on past conditions indicates lines of change within the one community. When I discussed an institution with old people they usually described it as it had worked when they were young. Many institutions I saw functioning both as described by old people and in modified forms. The most intelligible way of presenting very complex material seems to be to give an account of a custom or institution as I have seen it functioning in conservative families, or as it has been described to me by old people, and then to discuss how it is now being modified..." (p. 13)

The reasons for including descriptions of an urban native community in this study of native life and of the existence of the natives on European farms, are also given:

"The nature and degree of European influence has, however, varied in different areas, and an attempt has been made to study the changes taking place in comparing Bantu communities in three areas —reserves, towns, and European-owned farms—which have been subject to different contact influence. These communities are not an evolutionary series, for not only the degree, but the nature of the contact in each area differs, yet the background of each community is the same, and a comparison affords some indication of the lines of change resulting from contact."

A certain resemblance is to be discerned between this approach and that of Redfield in attacking the problem of cultural change in Mexico. The resemblance is not a close one; furthermore, the two presentations cannot be compared in the extent to which the philosophy underlying the methods employed by the two students has been given clarity of statement. But both of these investigations are none the less marked by reluctance to utilize historic data alone when attempting to explain the changes that have occurred in the societies they study, and hence both seek a method whereby the dynamics of the situation can be caught at first-hand instead of in retrospect.

The description of Pondo life as lived on the reserve takes the form of a conventional ethnographic study, giving in admirable detail the various aspects of the culture under consideration and only departing from the traditional mode of presentation by including under each heading a short discussion of the manner in which European influences are to be discerned. These influences, however, have in most cases almost to be deduced from the text, for despite the introductory statements that have been quoted, the evidences given of European influences on the aboriginal tribal life are so slight that one comes from the book with the impression that this tribe has preserved its earlier culture to a much greater extent than, for instance, have the BaKxatla. An objective measure of the extent to which culture has been but little effected by contact is found in the statistics of plural marriage (p. 202), a native institution that, as is well known, is invariably the subject of attack by Europeans:

No. of wives per man	1911 No. of men	1921 No. of men
1	187,864	194,376
2	21,490	20,321
3	2,857	2,500
4	594	390
5	168	121
from 6 to 20	93	67

The expressions of opinion concerning the need for reconstructing aboriginal life and the difficulties in the way of doing this that are found in the Introduction seem therefore to be in the nature of superfluous gestures toward a methodology the applicability of which to the tribe being studied is far from clear. As a matter of fact, the Pondo on their reserve live a life that, for the slightness of its acculturation to European civilization, does not seem comparable to that of a tribe of American Indians such as the Navajo, the aboriginal character of whose culture is constantly being stressed.

The greater part of the book, therefore, comprises an excellent monograph on the life of this primitive folk, with certain remarks concerning those of its institutions that have in some way been affected by contact with Europeans. Some of these remarks are not without value for the study of acculturation, especially where, as in the discussion of the Christian marriage ceremonial, a series of customs are presented in detail which "illustrate the fusion of Bantu and Christian ideas, and show some interesting 'emergent' ceremonies which exist in neither of the parent rituals, but which have grown out of the fusion of the two." (p. 23) But even here this must be taken for granted, or this result must be inferred from reference to the prior descriptions of aboriginal rites, for the ceremony is not analyzed so as to show which parts of it are native, which are European, and which are "emergent."

The second section discusses native life in the town of East London, where the Bantu population is composed principally of Pondo, Fingo, Xhosa and Thembu—tribes among whom, we are told, there are "no great differences," since all these people live not far from one another and there has been a considerable amount of intermarriage among them. "In the towns visited the people of the four tribes live mixed up, and intermarry, so that in a study of the community it was impossible to separate them." (p. 438) The technique employed here was naturally quite different than that used on the reserve. It perhaps closest resembles what is usually termed a sociological community study—the word "sociological" being here used in its American, and not its British sense. Statistics are given showing the numbers of those employed, by whom and in what capacities; the wages they earn; the number of rooms in which they live; and the manner in which their earnings are budgeted. An echo of life on the Reserve ends the discussion of the economic customs of these urban dwellers, where it is shown how in such matters as guarding against unemployment, or seeing to it that rooms available for rent in one's house are rented, or that one's shop will attract trade, the people turn to aboriginal magical practices. Against this economic setting of the life of this underprivileged group the other phases of their existence are projected, the whole being traced against the background of native custom described in detail in the first part of the book. The same procedure is adopted in the third section, which treats of native life on European farms.

These three principal parts are brought together in a final section headed "Tendencies," in which the changes that are occurring on the Reserve, on the farms and in the towns are considered together, and an attempt is made to assess future trends in the light of present movements. The portion of this section which is probably of greatest significance for an understanding of cultural change under the impact of foreign traditions is that in which is described how the natives in closest contact with the Europeans, who are thus subject most immediately to the discrimination practised in South Africa against those of non-European stock, tend to form defensive alliances and set up other contra-acculturative devices to meet the situation. Because of the prominence given such movements as the Ghost Dance Religion in the United States, and the various prophet movements in New Guinea and elsewhere, an assumption has grown that reaction to foreign domination must take the form of escape into other-worldliness. That this is only one alternative is made clear for, as far as South Africa is concerned, though there have been several revivalistic movements, the situation is for the most part being met by organizations of a politico-economic character which are much more concerned with meeting the realities of the present than with fleeing from those realities.

The approach attempted in this volume to the study of the processes of cultural change as they are working out in South Africa thus has certain potentialities for acculturation research, but much more work must be done before these potentialities can be realized. For not only does the final section quite fail to tie in with the material of the preceding parts of the book so that a dynamic portrayal of cultural changes in operation is afforded, but grave methodological lapses mar the conclusions. Thus it is superfluous to insist on a full and exact knowledge of an aboriginal culture as antecedent to an understanding of the changes resultant upon its contact with a foreign body of tradition if, in arranging a series of comparisons between these folk in their native habitat and away from home, people who do not even belong to the same tribe are used to establish the desired control. Yet it is just such a shift of base that confronts us in this book. In comparing the Reserve and urban dwellers, this fact has been recognized and, as has been quoted above, a defense of the procedure is made by indicating that the four tribes from which the urban population has come have similar cultures, while the urban population does, moreover, include a reasonable proportion of individuals who belong to the tribe studied on the Reserve. But in the case of the farm-workers what we find is that "the majority are Xhosa, but there are also Thembu, Fingo, and *a few* Pondo and Suto living on the same farms." (p. 505; italics inserted.) Should adequate controls be established along the lines suggested here, however, the method may yield findings of considerable importance for those concerned with cultural dynamics as operative in the contact of peoples and with the effect of contact on the human beings who undergo these experiences in changing cultures.

The studies that have thus far been discussed do not by any means exhaust the list of works that would merit inclusion in a complete survey; enough have been reviewed, however, to demonstrate the methods of studying acculturation that have been devised, and therefore other studies that have been made in East Africa, Australia, Melanesia, Polynesia, the East Indies, the Philippines, and the Asiatic mainland must be passed by with briefer notice. Some of these—most of them, as a matter of fact—are of less scientific usefulness to the student of cultural processes because their primary concern is with remedial programs or administrative problems. Yet there are some methodological suggestions and data of value to be found in them, especially as concerns those aspects of culture, such as political organization, where it is especially important to the administrator to have the most detailed information.

Thus Thurnwald's study of culture change in East Africa[1] includes historical analyses based on data drawn from "district books"— reports of officials who have had to deal with the tribes of the area —that represent a useful example of how unpromising sources can

[1] Thurnwald, (1935).

be employed to good advantage; the exercises written by native boys in European schools reveal a great deal concerning the attitudes of these young people that stem from the cultural confusion amid which they live. The use of questionnaires by Mrs. Thurnwald[1] is also an unusual adaptation of a device which, though its deficiencies can be granted, has proved of some value over the years it has been employed in studies made of our own culture. Yet, on the other hand, the work is marked by an attempt to do too much; too many tribes are considered, and too many different kinds of situations assessed; and there is too little of that directed attention to detail that is the sure path in scientific development. And while the book is almost the only work from the region that indicates the non-European acculturative forces operative there, and which pays some attention to the attitudes of Europeans toward natives; yet the importance of this approach is likewise vitiated by an eagerness not to offend those in power in describing the ends sought by them, and a tendency to inject evaluation where the facts might best speak for themselves.

It is this desire to make out a case for an administrative program that similarly lessens the usefulness of Mair's study of present-day life of the Baganda.[2] Again, the data are of value, but one must go through the book, noting down point after point in such a way as to reshuffle the materials in terms of the acculturative forces that have been at work, before the syncretizations that have resulted become apparent. No such analysis is made by the person best fitted to make it—the author—as, for example, Schapera has done in his consideration of the BaKxatla, or Parsons for the Mitleyenos.

Studies of culture contact in the islands of the Pacific, Australia, and New Guinea have been concerned with entire cultures only in a few instances, and in these the presentation has been too brief to allow an adequate description to be made of the life of the people

[1] *Ibid.*, Ch. IV and Appendix.
[2] Mair, (1934 b).

at the present time, let alone of their aboriginal culture. This again does not mean that publications useful to those concerned with scientific problems arising out of the study of cultural contact have not resulted from research in that region. The investigations that have been made into the contra-acculturative revivalistic movements of New Guinea that will be considered below are of the first rank; while from the pen of the same government anthropologist has come the most cogent and closely reasoned defense of the rôle of the anthropologist as an agent in directing change in the life of native peoples that has as yet appeared.[1] Here, also, work is being done that may well be the starting-point for studies in cultural contact that will not be haunted by Rivers' presupposition of the doom foreordained for primitive folk in contact with Europeans.[2] For as a result of working with Australian aborigines who have been most closely associated with Europeans over a long period of time, Elkin has discovered how much of their culture has survived.[3] From this experience he has developed his hypothesis of the three stages of adjustment which "from the point of view of the native race ... can frequently be distinguished in this history of its contact with immigrant white people"—"bewilderment, opposition, resentment, and a sense of loss ..."; scorn of the old days and "a feeling of inferiority with regard to their native culture" that may lead to depopulation unless a people can successfully pass through it; and finally "a return to the old faith, though somwhat modified, and a sense of worth regarding native arts, crafts, literature, law and custom ...."[4]

---

[1] Williams, (1935).

[2] Rivers' doctrine has recently been subjected to a vigorous attack by a non-anthropological writer (Harrisson, 1937) whose book, though unconventional in concept and presentation, gives much information of value on native-white contacts in the New Hebrides.

[3] Elkin, (1935).   [4] Elkin (1937), pp. 537–540.

All these studies thus enhance our knowledge of the results of contact and, as such, should be used by those concerned with acculturation. Though the principles that are adduced from such data are applicable only to current consequences of acculturation of native peoples to European norms of behavior, yet it must at least be recognized that they present no less a challenge than all those other speculative dicta that have issued in the past concerning the ways of human society in general. With such as these all anthropologists, whatever their particular interests or theoretical position, are familiar, and in testing generalizations concerning acculturation based only on native-European contacts ethnologists will be but once more performing the routine scientific service which in the past has characterized their work.

3

Studies of change in restricted phases of given cultures may be advantageously considered as well as in entire cultures, and there is much to be said in favor of the point of view that it is only through the detailed study of a single institution in a single culture that the dynamics of cultural change can be discerned. Granted that such studies require a knowledge of the range of patterns of the entire culture as background, this approach must nevertheless be recognized as having the inductive character that causes it to partake of the essence of scientific method.

It so happens that the most extensive analyses of change attendant on cultural contact studied in single institutions have had to do with religion. This is perhaps due in part to the striking nature of the revivalistic movements that have arisen among primitive peoples in contact with whites, which has caused them to stand out in bold relief against the background of their respective cultures, and has thus made them ready subjects for research. In the United States, the study of the Ghost Dance by Mooney, when it was still vigorous, made it natural for later students to devote further effort to this striking development, while the Peyote cult among the Indians, and the revivalistic movements of New Guinea and elsewhere have been singled out for treatment because their genesis and course of development among a given tribe could often be studied on the spot. In this section, then, studies of the various forms of revivalism among the American Indians known as the Prophet or Ghost Dance (except that of Mooney, which, though forming the basis of all later research, holds no particular significance for the study of acculturation either in theoretical statement or methodology), and investigations which deal with similar movements that developed in New Guinea, will be considered in some detail. Research in other special phases of single cultures will subsequently be reviewed more briefly.

a. Spier, Leslie, *The Prophet Dance of the Northwest.*

The supposition that the nativistic movements which since 1870 have appeared among the Indians of various parts of the United States constituted cults of despair, and represented reactions against social and political forces with which these natives could not cope, is sharply challenged in this paper. By means of elaborate documentation not only from ethnographic materials but from historic sources, what has been thought by many persons to have been a purely contra-acculturative phenomenon is shown actually to have arisen out of deep-seated aboriginal patterns which, even before the coming of the whites, had through intertribal acculturation come to be an integral part of the culture of at least the Indians of the Northwest, from whence the cult spread in its better-known revivalistic form first to California and then to the Plains.

The position taken can best be stated in the words of the author:

"It has been generally assumed that the Ghost Dance, which in 1890 spread throughout the Plains from a source in western Nevada, was a wholly new development engendered by the need for a messiah at the moment and without historically connected antecedents. Such was the stand taken by Mooney in his monumental work on the Ghost Dance cult. For him other messianic or prophetic movements among the Indians were merely so many parallels which, with similar activities among Old World peoples, provided some notion of the psychic milieu from which messianic movements sprang.

"It was known to Mooney that some twenty years earlier another prophet had appeared among the Paviotsos, whose doctrine was identical with that of Wovoka, the accredited Paviotso originator of the 1890 affair. But this antecedent development did not appear to Mooney to have any special significance. It remained for Kroeber to show that about 1870 a doctrine and dance having its source in this earlier Paviotso prophet swept westward through northern and central California as in 1890 the Ghost Dance swept eastward through the Plains....

"It is the purpose of this section of this paper to show that the ultimate origin of the two Ghost Dance movements was not with the Paviotso but in the Northwest among the tribes of the interior Plateau area. It can be shown that among these peoples there was an old belief in the impending destruction and renewal of the world, when the dead would return, in conjunction with which there was a dance based on supposed imitation of the dances of the dead, with a conviction that intense preoccupation with the dance would hasten the happy day.... This northwestern cult agrees precisely with the core of the Ghost Dance religion among the Paviotso, and the circumstances of its appearance among the latter parallel those of earlier date in the Northwest." (p. 5)

Because of the numerous forms taken by this revivalist cult in the various tribes to which it spread, the author coins the name "Prophet Dance" as a generic term for it.

It is not necessary for our purpose to follow the argument in detail. What may be emphasized is that the author in documenting his thesis has made an important contribution to the study of acculturation, both as a corrective for the too facile approach that assumes that anything which bears resemblance to European custom must, where native folk have been in contact with individuals or groups of European affiliation, be derived from this source, and as an instance of a process of intertribal acculturation that continued as a result of long and intimate contact between tribes which, in the aggregate, covered a wide area.

Because the influence of Christianity has been so stressed in discussions of Prophet Dance sects, it is important to note that most of its elements can be derived from aboriginal customs. Thus among the Northern Okanagon of Oregon there was a confession dance "held whenever some strange natural happening was felt to portend the end of the world," and Murdock is quoted to the effect that "public confession was also incorporated in the Smohalla rites of the Tenino" and that "the informant insisted that confession was aboriginal, not borrowed from Christianity." The insistence on proselytizing which marks these cults has also been referred to Christianity, yet "though this is a most unusual characteristic for an Indian cult," there is valid reason to doubt its Christian origin since "it seems to be involved in the very nature of the [Ghost Dance] doctrine" and since there is "specific documentation for it in the Northwest as a pre-Christian practice." (p. 12)

Not only is there testimony from the Northwest that the elements of the Prophet Dance were present before the coming of the whites, but similar evidence is found in the Southern Plateau and the Great Basin regions. For though the historical material is fragmentary, what does exist seems to indicate that its Christian-like aspects were already there when the earliest travellers reached the region. (p. 19) That some Christian elements were introduced between the time of these first voyagers and their successors seems apparent, but they were merely incorporated into pre-existing forms of native custom:

"The travellers of the eighteen-thirties give evidence only for the externals of native practice. What the doctrinal background of the rites may have been, whether wholly Christian or pagan, or a blend, we do not know. They assumed that the rites were perverted Christian forms—certainly the observance of the Sabbath and calendric holidays, and the posture in prayer are clearly Christian—so that we must take their word for it. On the other hand fully half the ritual elements described as incorporated in the compound correspond to known native forms." (p. 20)

Though it is thus apparent that the Prophet Dance was firmly established in the patterns of native culture before contact with whites took place, it must not be inferred that later acculturation with European forms of religious belief did not occur. What is demonstrated in the initial sections of this monograph is that when these European traits did arrive, concepts and rituals that might afford a hospitable matrix into which the new customs and beliefs could efficiently lodge were already present. It is with this in mind that we pass to the later sections of this work, which deal with the early Christianized versions of the Prophet Dance (1820–1836), and the Smohalla and Shaker cults.

The derivation of the former is "sufficiently romantic," resulting, as it did, from the influence exerted by a "band of Iroquois, twenty-four men, who about 1829 found a new home for themselves among the Flathead in the mountains of Montana." These Indians, who perhaps had left Quebec "during those troublous times following the defeat of the Iroquois as partisans of the British in the war of 1812–14," introduced their new neighbors to the concepts and practices of Catholicism. And since, as a Catholic historian who is quoted says, "the ties of friendship soon ripened into stronger ones by intermarriage," an unusual form of secondary acculturation took place wherein inter-Indian contact was the medium through which the religion of the whites was brought to a group of Indians as yet unaffected by it.

Yet here again it must be remembered that as far as the recipients were concerned, the acculturation that occurred was a process that was essentially congenial to the old patterns. As the matter is phrased:

"The fact is that the Christian forms which the travellers of the eighteen-thirties encountered west of the Rockies were compounded with the native Prophet cult. Further, it would seem that it was the prior existence of the Prophet Dance which explains both the ready acceptance of Christianity at its point of introduction and its rapid spread." (p. 30)

Once introduced among the Flathead, this Christianized series of rituals spread through contact between the tribes of the region, and numerous quotations from contemporary explorers and others attest to its presence at dates that again preclude first-hand white influence:

"We have direct evidence for it among the Flathead, Nez Perce, Cayuse, and Walla Walla; we may infer it for their immediate Salish and Sahaptin neighbors; and we know that it reached as far south as the Shoshoni in southern Idaho and west to the Upper Chinook or Sahaptins of the Dalles. With the historians we have every reason to believe that the Christian elements were introduced by the Iroquois of Montana." (p. 35)

The reasons why Christian belief and the "prior Prophet cult" should have been amalgamated so harmoniously, and with enough cohesion so that the new religion could spread as a unit from its place of origin, are given in the following passage:

"The doctrines are parallel; the rites are not in conflict. Both tell of an apocalyptic end with the return to earth of its pristine happiness and the resurrection of the dead, the way prepared by a righteous life and a strict adherence to devotions; in both prophets bring affirmation. That they actually amalgamated rites rather than made a substitution is attested by the evidence. So far as the natives were concerned then the new religion from the east was confirmation and stimulus to existing beliefs." (p. 35)

Relatively little is known of the Smohalla and the Shaker religions, but enough information is available to show that both are "good Prophet Dance" despite the fact that in them Christian elements are prominent to a far greater degree than is the case with the other forms that have been considered. The Smohalla cult, which "made its appearance among the Sahaptin tribes of the interior perhaps in the eighteen-sixties or earlier," is "most certainly a direct offshoot of the [Prophet] cult of the eighteen-thirties." "The Shaker religion, avowedly a Christian cult, was almost certainly affected at its origin by the Smohalla revival, although there is a somewhat remote possibility that some of its roots lie still farther back in the original form of the Prophet Dance." The date for the introduction of this religion is 1882; spreading southward from southern Puget Sound, it has flourished and is "one of the principal faiths of the Indians of the coastal district." (p. 40)

The Smohalla cult takes its name from that of its "prophet," and manifests the results of acculturation to Christianity in its ritual, rather than in its doctrine, which is quite in accord with the tenets of the Prophet faith that preceded it. Though the elements of this can be analyzed to reveal their provenience from Christian as well as from pagan beliefs and rites, it is held that instead of being derived from missionaries, its roots rather lie in "the less pagan portions of the 1830 rites." Hence despite the fact that ". . . there can be little question that mission experience affected Smohalla or whoever was responsible for the configuration of 1860–70, . . the ultimate source. . . appears to be the brand of Christianity brought in by the Iroquois of Montana." (p. 45)

The Shaker religion, which is "nominally Christian," also differs from the preceding one in that it is "an extraordinary blend of old shamanistic performances with Catholic ritual and Protestant doctrine." (p. 49) Originating in 1882 in the vision experience of one John Slocum, who "died" and, on being refused admission to Heaven

because of his wickedness, returned to preach the good life, its ceremonialism centers about three kinds of rites: church services, curing
the sick, and grace at meals. Perhaps more than any of these cults, it
is at once the agent and the object of further acculturative processes,
not only because the automobile permits much visiting between cult-
members of different tribes, but also because "in recent years they
have found a sympathetic bond with various sects of whites (Holy
Rollers, Seven-Day Adventists), and more recently, on Klamath
Reservation and in northwestern California have made friendly
contact with the Four-Square Gospel hailing from southern California." (p. 54)

b. Gayton, A. H., *The Ghost Dance of 1870 in South-Central California.*

This description of the spread of the 1870 Ghost Dance to the
Yokuts-Mono peoples of central California may be regarded as
complementary to the more general treatment that has just been
discussed, though it preceded this other by several years. The methodology of the two studies is identical, for both collate information
obtained in the field with materials from historical sources.

Whether or not this particular revivalistic movement resulted from
breakdown in native culture due to white contact is not clear. Two
comments throw some light on the point; the first being a quotation
from Stephen Powers' "The Tribes of California":

"He [Old Sam, who probably brought the Ghost Dance of 1870 to
the Miwok] counseled them to live at peace with the whites, to treat
them kindly, and to avoid quarrels whenever possible, as it was worse
than useless to contend against their conquerors." (p. 65, n. 1)

The second is a comment on the site of the great Eshom Valley
Dance of 1872:

"This spot was selected because of its central location in the lower
mountains and its seclusion from the white settlers." (p. 69)

The absence of a demonstrated connection between the situation of the Indians in the face of an advancing frontier and the revivalism under discussion may, however, be due to the specialized focus of this paper. A paragraph bearing on the point may be cited:

"What the relations were between the Indians of the San Joachim Valley and the white population of 1870 is not clear from native accounts. The statement of one informant that 'after that the white man came' leads one to believe that the number of white settlers before that time was negligible. The Indians of the San Joachim plains were the first to suffer the loss of life, lands, and hence of economic liberty; those living in the foothills where the Ghost Dance was first introduced were as yet scarcely disturbed .... Even so the natives may have been disconcerted by the white man's continued approach. No informant will admit that the messianic faith had any reference to the presence of the white people, much less that hostile intentions toward the whites lurked beneath the Ghost Dance activities. Whether or not this was so can scarcely be proved now." (pp. 80-81)

The mechanism which made for the spread of the movement—the established formula that persons from "adjacent tribes" might attend and take part in any dances—was thus one of acculturation, whatever the influence of contact with white culture may have been. Moreover, "it is seen that...the social system and certain ritual elements of the Ghost Dance...were entirely in consonance with established procedure at intertribal celebrations" (p. 77), while the concepts which made up the ideological foundation of the movement were also in harmony with earlier patterns.

Yet if this were entirely the case, the study of the Ghost Dance among these tribes would present no problem for us; hence it is important to note that in such aspects of the ritual as all-night dancing, the fact that the taboo against eating meat during a ceremony was not observed in the Ghost Dance, the restoration of persons having spells to consciousness by the chiefs rather than by shamans, and the non-payment of the singer accompanists (pp. 78–79), there were important elements of the ritual that "varied from the San Joachim norm."

The matter is thus summarized:

"The process of acculturation is evident from our detailed account of Ghost Dances at Saganiu and Eshom valley. Analysis of the social background into which the new cult was thrust indicates that the social process involved in holding dances ... was entirely in the order of the established system for intertribal ceremonials. Several features of the Ghost Dance doctrine were interpreted in terms of extant cultural forms....Analagous acculturations are found among the Klamath and in northwest California. The doctrine of the Ghost Dance which promised the return of dead relatives, absolution from sickness or death, a continuous life of peace and prosperity, is ubiquitous in its human appeal. This, together with the fact that the cult had no complex features of belief and was open for collective participation, made it uniquely suitable for a rapid diffusion regardless of the type of culture encountered in its travels. The framework and stimulus of the revivalistic cult were supplied, the details were filled in according to the individual taste of varying culture patterns." (p. 82)

Finally, in this connection, the manner in which the Dance was accepted by these people is clarified by considering its later rejection in the light of the dominant patterns:

"The abandonment of the Ghost Dance was not due to pressure exerted by the white population but rather to disillusionment. The closing words of Takac's address were quite in keeping with the philosophical outlook of the Yokuts-Mono mind. Their past life was a singularly placid and pleasant one. They were not ridden by a mass of superstitious fears as are many primitive peoples. There were few taboos; no religious office or supernatural function was imposed on anyone who did not want it. Individuals went about their daily lives following the simple rules of their religious and social order without burdening themselves with taboos and privations, believing that if the supernatural powers wished to help them they would. The same attitude is expressed in the resolution of their feelings toward the messianic cult. Exhaustive efforts to bring back their 'father' and their dead relatives had proved to be futile, hence, give it up—'if that man is coming, he'll come anyway'." (p. 81)

c. Nash, Philleo, *The Place of Religious Revivalism in the Formation of the Intercultural Community of Klamath Reservation.*[1]

This paper supports a position concerning the reasons for the rise of revivalistic movements among native folk in contact with whites which opposes that advanced concerning the same phenomenon in the preceding contributions. Noting that such revivals are "remarkably uniform in doctrine despite the dissimilarity of the cultures in which they appear," that "they are not mere importations of Christian dogma," but that "on the contrary, they usually rest firmly on aboriginal religious beliefs, which have been reworked and reintegrated in a manner which gives an appearance of uniformity," an initial hypothesis, based on the consideration of such movements in the United States, New Guinea and India, was nevertheless formulated in the following terms:

"Nativistic cults arise among deprived groups. They follow a shift in the value pattern, due to suppression and domination, and are movements to restore the original value pattern which they do by the construction of a fantasy situation. The nature of this fantasy, which is basic to the cult, is a function of (1) the original value pattern and (2) the successive changes in the value pattern under white domination." (pp. 377–378)

Thus a group that has been deprived of its power is held to compensate for its impotence by setting up cults which, in doctrine and ritual, offer to the members of the deprived group opportunities to identify themselves with some power that is sufficiently great to cope with the

[1] The exerpts from this paper are reproduced here with the kind permission of the University of Chicago press, publishers of the volume wherein it appeared.

situation, and sufficiently friendly to support their cause. In its early form, this envisages a return to the "good old days"; as time goes on, the picture of these "good old days" in the minds of the people becomes warped by the acculturation to which they are subjected, and hence takes on a somewhat different form, incorporating foreign values.

The hypothesis was tested by field-work on the Klamath Reservation, where the nativistic revivalist movement of 1871–1878 was studied. In 1864, three tribes were brought together on this reservation; the Klamath, whose home territory it had been, the Modoc, who gave armed resistance to attempts to transfer them, and the Paviotso, who vacillated between their aboriginal habitat and the reservation for many years in a state of "passive resistance" until they finally settled on it. The first two of these tribes were relatively similar in culture and language, but the Paviotso differed considerably in both.

"If the hypothesis is correct, those groups which participated most fully in the revival should be those which suffered most deprivation in their contacts with whites. Furthermore, the fantasy situation integral to the cult should be appropriate to shifts in the value pattern which had taken place in the formation of the intercultural community." (p. 378)

The question in point is "broken down into two problems"—that of "deprivation" and that of "participation in the religious revival." (pp. 378–379) Before taking up these matters, however, an analysis is made of the historical setting of the movement in terms of "the formation of the intercultural community."

Changes in the life of the three tribes when they were "put on the reservation" appear to have been essentially internal ones; more in the nature of shifts of emphasis—at least as far as the Klamath were concerned—in the social position of chiefs, shamans, commoners and slaves:

"In general, the formation of the intercultural community on the Upper End [of the reservation] was characterized by independence and absence of restraint, by few contacts with whites, by minimal cultural changes, and by the formation of a compact community rather than the scattered type of the Lower End.

"The formation of the intercultural community on both ends of the reservation was characterized by early and simple beginnings of cultural change. Acceptance of white customs and techniques was barely under way in this first ten years of administrative control. Ten years later many more changes had taken place, but in the period under consideration the Indians depended on the collection of wild foods in their original habitat, to a large extent, and had taken over certain superficial characteristics of white culture, but the basic change to dependence on individual enterprise in the form of one-family subsistence farms, with reliance on agriculture and grazing techniques, was common only in the last half of the period, and only at the Lower End. The most notable feature is that the Indians accepted the changes eagerly and industriously, only to find that their efforts met with failure, through no fault of their own." (pp. 406–407)

The effects of the exposure to white domination on these three tribes is thus stated:

"...with respect to two factors in change, the groups on the Klamath Reservation were aligned as follows: (1) with respect to initial deprivation the Modoc suffered most, the Klamath suffered least, and the Paviotso were intermediate; (2) with respect to changes introduced through administrative policy and attendant deprivation and indulgence, the Klamath changed most, the Paviotso least, while the Modoc were intermediate." (p. 412)

This background of change and resistance to change established, the facts concerning the revivalistic movement are then analyzed. Three phases of its development are distinguished, the Ghost Dance, the Earthlodge cult, and the Dream Dance. It is noted that of the three tribes the Modoc who, at the time of the introduction of the cult,

were seething with revolt against the plan to place them on reservation
—a state of mind that later resulted in the "Modoc war"—adopted
the first phase most readily, and was the only group to attach to it an
aspect of violence. And it is pointed out that this is in line with what
might have been expected in the light of the historic rôle of the
Modoc:

"The inclusion of the collective symbol and the doctrinal stress on
the dead, coupled with extremely aggressive elements in the doctrine,
are consonant with the damage to the collective symbol suffered by
contact with whites." (p. 418)

In contrast, the interest of the Klamath in the dance was limited both
in time and degree; among the Paviotso, it was merely a "religious
revival in a strict sense; an increase in religious activity accompanied
by the enhancement of well-established symbols and practices."
(p. 420)

With the onset of the Earthlodge stage greater emphasis was placed on
the individual, while the earlier elements of pugnacity were removed;
the cult offered more of a personal escape from a situation that was
distasteful, while it also afforded prestige to commoners and slaves
who, in aboriginal society, could not have hoped to attain a like
position. As this phase passed into the Dream Dance, worship
became still more highly "personalized" and, though associated with
the dead, no longer envisaged their return to earth. Dreams required
interpretation, and for this the members of the cult would seek out
the shamans, so that as this phase was ended by the oncoming of
Christianity the cycle back to the shaman as the most significant
figure in the manipulation of the supernatural had been completed.
In this cycle only the Indian employees of the agency, whose desire
for prestige and a place in the scheme of things had been satisfied,
took no part but even attempted at one time to suppress the movement.

In essence, these data tend to show that those who suffered most under the initial impact of white contact compensated most for it. The findings of field research, on which this paper is based, made it desirable to revise the initial hypothesis, and this was restated in the following manner:

"Nativistic cults arise among deprived groups. Deprivation may occur within the framework of either acceptance or rejection of values and skills associated with white culture. Revivalism, however, is only one aspect of a total response to white culture. Revivalism is that portion of the response which expresses in ritual symbolism the basic attitudes of acceptance or rejection of white culture, feelings of loss or damage, aggressive retaliation in response to deprivation suffered, and self-punishing assertions and practices in proportion to aggressive retaliation." (p. 442)

A number of points may be raised which bear on this treatment as related to the study of acculturation in general. Granting that the shock of initial conflict incident on native-white contacts causes compensatory movements, it is unfortunate that one fundamental aspect of this phenomenon, so often stressed in this paper—the formation of what is called the "intercultural community"—is nowhere treated as its importance deserves. What confronts us again and again is the familiar overemphasis on white influence. Thus, on page 404, the isolation of the "Upper End" community from whites is explicitly pointed out. Or, on page 410, the statement "Jack's group, of course, was not subject to *the acculturation policy*"[1] implies that the term "acculturation" is appropriate only when elements of white culture are taken over by natives. Another passage indicates how stress on white influence tends to warp the description of the situation:

"The reservation Modoc were subject to the same initial deprivation as the Tule Lake Modoc. They suffered additional damage to

[1] Italics inserted.

the group symbol at the hands of a non-white group—the Klamath....
The fact that no anti-Klamath doctrine appears fixes the character
of the revival as an anti-white movement. There was an anti-Klamath
reaction, non-ritual in its nature, which, aside from the flight to the
Lost River, took the form of gossip and hostile anecdotes which are
remembered to this day."

And though this paper is concerned primarily with revivalism, yet
it must be regarded as regrettable that the identification of the word
"acculturation" with "adaptation to white modes of life" has apparently not permitted the author to see that compensatory mechanisms
in non-ritualized form are, for his very problem, just as significant
as those which do take ritual form.

There are other instances where lack of clarity has made for confusion, as where the author states: "...we may now proceed to that
aspect of cultural change which seems most closely connected with
deprivation—religious revivalism." (p. 412) Quite aside from the
question of the advisability of using "cultural change" as a synonym
for "acculturation," it is doubtful whether the available materials on
culture contact would support the implied assumption. It has been
seen how among the South African Bantu other mechanisms of
adjustment are quite as prevalent as religious ones; while among the
Bushmen and Hottentots, who have suffered far more "deprivations"
than the Indians treated in this paper, we find no evidence of any
kind of religious revivalism.

d. Lesser, Alexander, *The Pawnee Ghost Dance Hand Game.*

This volume treats the development of one special phase of a
local variant of the 1890 Ghost Dance. The work is not only significant for the study of acculturation because, as the author states, the
data are such as to leave "no residue" of material for further study,
but the research is also important from the point of view of method,
since it repersents a "typical case of controlled cultural transform-

ation..." where "the method of exhaustive analysis supported by historical background has demonstrated with exactitude the origins and influences of change." (p. 321)

The discussion begins with a thorough account of the vicissitudes of the Pawnee in their original habitat in Nebraska, as the frontier moved westward and took with it any chance for continued stability of aboriginal life. This prompted the removal of the tribe on their own volition to Oklahoma, where a friendly related folk, the Wichita, were already living and where there was hope of better days. This hope, however was not to be realized, so that by 1892, when the Ghost Dance spread to them, they "had come to a cultural impasse, with nothing to look forward to and nothing to live by." (p. 52)

This dance came to the Pawnee through the instrumentality of one Frank White, "a Pawnee Indian who was among the southern Oklahoma tribes who were Ghost dancing; he participated in dances among the Comanche and Wichita, learned the doctrine, and observed the early forms in which the dancing was at that time organized..." (p. 57) Despite the conversions he made to the new doctrine, his arbitrary control of the rites and his use of the Ghost Dance for personal gain brought on discontent, so that late in 1892 a democratization of the ritual occurred, and the cult was reintroduced in the form which it now takes.

It may be well at this point to summarize in the author's words the hope held out to the Indians by the Ghost Dance doctrine when, as a result of "the United States government program of assimilation" the Pawnee found that "their old life was gone, and nothing adequate had been given them in its place." The new ritual "promised the coming of a new and restored Indian earth, on which the white man would be no more, and on which the buffalo would roam again"; it "prescribed the casting aside of the white man's ways as an expression of faith"; and, in its third tenet, which "concerned the visions and the seeking of them," it offered "moments of intercommunication between those here on earth and their deceased kinsmen in the beyond," which were a medium through which one could "prove one's strength of faith" and could foresee what "the new earth was to be like." (p. 105) It was thus clearly a contra-acculturative movement, and it is not difficult to understand its appeal to the Indians; especially when it is realized how deeply its rites lodged in aboriginal pattern:

"The revival of Pawnee culture which began to materialize in the years of the Ghost Dance went back for its material primarily to three sources in the old culture: the bundles and bundle rituals, the societies, and the games. The general attempt to resuscitate the aboriginal forms, supplemented and fortified by the inspirations and mandates of the visions, resulted in three types of cultural rebirth. The activities of old ceremony, performance and play were fostered; the paraphernalia were put in order, renewed, and recreated; and concepts from the old context were enshrined in symbols and facsimiles which were carried in the dance and integrated into new cultural forms." (p. 106)

The setting for this reintegration was provided by the new freedom which governmental policy gave the Pawnee, together with the fact that they "found themselves side by side with white men for the first time in their history" as a result of the allotment system which broke up the reservation and, in addition to contact with whites, had a counter effect of enhancing the importance of opportunities for communal gatherings. (pp. 119–123)

With the setting, historical, geographical, and cultural thus in hand, the author devotes the second portion of his work to an intensive consideration of the hand game itself, both in its aboriginal form and as concerns its present rôle as a part of the Ghost Dance ceremonies. His analysis includes a description of the paraphernalia employed in the game in pre-white days and at present, the differences in the social setting of the game in earlier times and now, changes in the behavior of the participants, as well as the obvious matter of the changes as the game was transformed from one devoted to purposes of gambling to one that is part of a religious rite. Its inclusion in the Ghost Dance is shown to have come subsequent to the elimination of White as the sole prophet, when the validity of individual vision experiences was affirmed; a development which so flourished "as late as 1930," that the author tells us he "was able to list twenty-two individual game developments of the Pawnee." (p. 155)

In the detailed analyses of the various forms of the games as revealed in visions, relatively little of European practice or belief is to be seen. In the "church games" there are obvious influences, such as the intervals between bouts of guessing, when "Forty-Nine or Soldier songs" are sung, or where a Baptist recites a prayer before the play instead of giving the conventional smoke-offering, or when grace is said before the food is eaten instead of the aboriginal food-offering, but there is little more than this. In the vast majority of forms of the hand game no Christian ritual occurs, and European influences are confined to identifications of Christian concepts with early modes of thought and practice.

This detailed description of the forms taken by the games in accordance with the revelations had by their "owners" is followed by a discussion of how traits of the older form have been retained or lost and of how those added to the game have been worked into the complex as it now exists. Such an analysis is in accordance with the methodology of the author in utilizing this game as a form with which to document "under control" a specific example of cultural change:

"The persistence of traits constitutes that body of cultural elements without which no identification of the two forms would be possible. There are first of all those traits which persist from the old game into the new form identically; these form the base. In addition there are persistences of phases of the pattern or form, into which similar but not identical cultural material has been filled." (p. 309)

This "base" of persisting traits is seen to be considerable—those "for the most part...associated with the actual play of the game" (p. 309), while those lost derive from its aspects that came from the identification of the play with the imagery of the war party. Finally, in analyzing the traits added to the original complex, we are permitted clearly to see here, as elsewhere in the book, the operation of that process of revamping that is so fundamental to cultural change in any of its manifestations.

e. Chinnery, E. P. W. and Haddon, A. C., *Five New Religious Cults in British New Guinea.*

This paper gives a sense of the underlying pattern of those outbreaks of religious hysteria in New Guinea which, because of their widespread nature and frequent occurrence, must be taken into account in discussing the rise of similar more recent manifestations in this area. At the same time, it offers some of the few available instances of intertribal acculturation.

The first two cults, which are briefly described by Chinnery, are each founded on the worship of a "Food-Spirit." Despite governmental action in putting down their overt forms, they were continuing underground at the time of writing and were threatening to "break out in strong force along the whole northern coast from the Gira to Buna at any time." (p. 451) How they have developed from their beginnings cannot be stated, since no further reports concerning them have been published.

Haddon's contribution to this joint paper gives an account of the origin and forms of three more cults and, in addition, makes generalizations on the basis of his data. In the light of his own later descriptions, his statement that the cults described by Chinnery "do not seem to be related to the somewhat earlier cult to which I call attention, nor is there any evidence of the slightest connection between these and the abortive message of the Milne Bay 'prophet'" tends to underline the rôle of the cultural base in making possible these messianic movements. This is further emphasized by the notes on the cult of Mansoren Korēri among the tribes of Netherlands New Guinea given by Moszkowski[1] which, as Haddon remarks, is not unlike similar cults in the British portion of the island in that it envisages the culture-hero as a person who, disappointed that the tribe failed to carry out his injunctions, vanished and is believed destined to return "and then everything will be renewed."

The problem of the relation of these cults to white encroachment on native custom is considered by Haddon in his preliminary remarks:

"An awakening of religious activity is a frequent characteristic of periods of social unrest. The weakening or disruption of the older social order may stimulate new and often bizarre ideals, and these may give rise to religious movements that strive to sanction social or political aspirations. Communities that feel themselves oppressed anticipate the emergence of a hero who will restore their prosperity and prestige. And when the people are imbued with religious fervour the expected hero will be regarded as a Messiah. Phenomena of this kind are well known in history, and are not unknown at the present day among peoples in all stages of civilization." (p. 455)[2]

The reference made to the Ghost Dance of North America as a similar messianic contra-acculturative movement would come to mind were it not mentioned by the authors in this connection.

Nonetheless, we are told that even without the disruption of native custom by white interference, movements of a similar revivalistic nature are known to have occurred—movements which are of importance for the ethnologist's understanding of the dynamics of culture from an entirely different point of view than that being stressed here, but are of no less significance for us because of this fact:

[1] Moszkowski (1911), p. 327.
[2] In much of this Haddon takes a position which was to be assumed by Nash two decades later.

"...even among the savages of New Guinea fresh forms of religious activity come into being from time to time definitely as a reaction against the encroachments of the white man. But the mainspring of others is at present obscure, and appears to be more distinctly related to purely native ideas. These cults afford a valid ground of argument against the very prevalent notion of the permanence of all native institutions.... They illustrate...the methods by which cults have probably spread in the past, and, as I have previously suggested [referring here to a statement in the Reports of the Cambridge Anthropological Expedition to Torres Straits] we have evidence elsewhere of a definite propaganda. Indeed, we might... admit that savages may occasionally have a missionary zeal which impels them to impart to the benighted heathen the ceremonial or cult that yields to themselves so much satifsaction." (pp. 455-456)[1]

Of the three religious movements described, the Baigona cult consists of serpent worship, administered by initiates deriving their knowledge from one Maine, to whom the original vision that began the cult was vouchsafed. The Prophet of Milne Bay was named Tokerua, and he foretold an early destruction of the world as it now exists and a return to the golden age. A number of natives destroyed their gardens at his behest, but when the "prophet" was imprisoned and the millenium failed to arrive, the cult collapsed. The third movement, that of the German Wislin of Saibai (Torres Straits) was also based on a doctrine of the return of the dead, and—in this strikingly like the Vailala Madness and the Kekesi cult—they were to return on a steamer, when they would fight and kill the white man. Certain Christian elements in the ritual and belief are seen to be "interwoven...with racial animosity and a recrudescence of the vague ancestor cult of heathen times" in all these cults (p. 463). However, it is not believed that borrowing was the cause of resemblances of this kind—certainly not those between the German Wislin of Saibai and

---

[1] Cf. the discussion of this point by Williams (1928), pp. 5-6 and 77ff.

the beliefs of the prophet of Milne Bay, since the two localities are 560 miles apart. "I think we can confidently attribute the coincidences to the fact that the two fishing populations have been affected in an analagous manner by the social unrest, and have also been more or less imbued with the Christian religion...." (pp. 462–463)

f. Williams, F. E., *The Vailala Madness and the Destruction of Native Ceremonies in the Gulf Division.*[1]

The "Vailala Madness" represents another of these New Guinea contra-acculturative movements which, on the surface, are strangely like the Prophet Dances of the American Indians. In both cases, apparently, the new cults arose as reactions to the hopelessness of the situation in which natives found themselves when faced with white agression; in both they were based on doctrines of the early return of the dead, and involved prophets, possession, and dancing; in both white rituals were copied to some extent; while finally, both movements seem to have run a swift course to an early and almost complete disappearance.

Here, however, the resemblance ends. In many parts of the United States the Ghost Dances were essentially anti-white and predicted the day when olden times would return and the invaders would be wiped out, a doctrine which in the Plains led to actual warfare. In Papua, however, though the doctrine was anti-white, the particular form discussed in this paper brought about the destruction of rituals and sacred objects of earlier times, and for these this new cult substituted a considerable number of Christian and secular European elements. In this, of course, it contrasts strikingly with the Ghost Dance, where the elements derived from the whites were few when compared to

---

[1] Reference should also be made to Williams, (1928). The titles analyzed here were selected because, in the case of the Vailala Madness, repeated observations over a period of time are available.

the number that consisted essentially of elaborations of certain aspects of the pattern already long established before contact with the whites.

The Vailala Madness is named after a town on the southern coast of New Guinea, on the Gulf of Papua, where the movement began during the latter months of 1919. Its commencement can be accurately dated, because the disturbance it caused was brought to the attention of a political officer who sent in careful reports concerning it. It was a dance involving "crazy, uncontrolled excitement" and "where it touched it made a clean sweep of ceremonies, and...destroyed almost every treasure of religion and art." (pp. 1-2) It spread up and down the coast and, to a lesser degree, into the interior up the Vailala River. One striking characteristic was its "spotty" distribution, so that one village, unaffected by it, might have a neighbor not more than a mile or two removed described as a "veritable hot-bed" of the cult.

The doctrine of the Madness centered about two principal tenets; the immediate return of the dead, and the belief that in the ancestral world all are white. The deceased relatives were expected to come in a large steamer, which was to be loaded with cases of gifts, and, in some early versions of the cult, was also to have on board cases of rifles to be used in driving the whites from the land; but these beliefs had short tenure. As to the ancestors being white, it is pointed out that this involved two concepts; "that the white men are the returned ancestors of the natives" and that "the natives become white in after-life"—two ideas which are not necessarily related. Beliefs of this type were not without their aboriginal sanction:

"As far back as 1912 a member of the London Missionary Society found the natives of Moviavi on one occasion in a state of the highest excitement because they had got hold of the idea that he himself was one of their returned ancestors.... The other belief...that in an after-life the black men will be white men, is common enough in the Gulf Division, and might easily be the result of Missionary influence, whether taught or not." (pp. 16-17)

Many Christian elements marked the doctrine. Heaven was called *Ihova Kekere* or "Jehova's Land," and Jesus, God, and other Christian designations were often encountered. "Some of the most prominent figures have declared that they were 'Jesus Christ men'" and implied that they would no longer follow heathen ways. "Certain of these men had, and still have, visions of God or Christ, from whom they receive instructions or messages for their fellows, usually of an ethical character." Similarly, the belief that the dead ascend into Heaven —the Christian Heaven, in the sky—was fundamental, while the ethical teachings of the cult—"Thou shalt not steal, commit adultery, nor break the Sabbath are the three commandments most frequently heard"—also argued Christian influence, as did the stress laid on the fact that all feasts should be shared equally by women and men, something quite out of line with earlier custom. (pp. 18–19, 24–26.)

These beliefs seem to have been an overlay, however, on the cult of the ancestors, which had long been present in the region:

"The really fundamental fact in the whole cult is the tremendous interest in the dead: and perhaps the most important regular duty connected with it is the making of mortuary feasts.... There is nothing new in the fact of these mortuary feasts in the Gulf Division; they are apparently part of the old culture; and they illustrate this keenly-felt interest in, and, to some extent, fear of the dead or rather of the spiritual entity that is believed to survive death. It would be a surprising thing if a new cult could abolish an interest so deeply grounded. Thus it would appear to be only in the highly pretentious style of arraying the feast that there has been any great deviation from former custom." (pp. 19–20)

Moreover, it is by no means as certain as would seem on the face of it that the Vailala Madness affected other aspects of native culture than the religious ones, granting it "wiped out" the earlier rites to the degree that is stressed. Thus, in the cult-houses where the "Head-he-go-round Men" officiated, there were separate tables allotted to the different clans or bark-cloth strips in the appropriate places with the emblems of the various clans to which they belonged. "Such facts," runs the comment, "indicate that the social organization has to some extent survived the Vailala Madness, or has been adapted to it...."

The cult of the dead, the heart of the Madness, consisted of mortuary feasts, food offerings to the dead, and communication with the dead. The most striking adoptions from European custom were made in connection with this aspect of the movement. Each village had its *ahea uvi*—"hot house"—where the Automaniacs became "hot" or possessed on entering, and where the rendezvous between the souls of the dead and these possessed ones took place. Before each house was a flag-pole "which seems to have been instituted by the London Missionary Society a good many years ago" from which a flag was especially flown on Sundays "when [it was] partly meant as a sign that the day should be kept." At the time of writing, however, it functioned "to permit certain individuals to receive messages from the dead through its agency"—and here comes perhaps the most up-to-date instance of acculturation that has been recorded —since the derivation of this use of the flag-pole, carefully traced, is shown to have been the wireless stations observed by natives at the coast and on shipboard! (p. 24)

Still other Europeanisms seem to have been adopted because of a desire to imitate the white man. The dead, for example, "are not infrequently depicted as clothed in European garments. One informant...was visited by God himself...wearing coat, shirt, trousers, hat and 'foot' and addressing him in the white man's tongue." Other examples given of this are the tendency to crop the hair close, the "fall-in" demanded of the villagers by those in charge, the regulation of dancing by whistle-blasts, and the institutions of the old nine o'clock curfew in Motu-Motu. (p. 25)

The origin of the Madness is said to have been the result of a sermon about the Resurrection preached by a white missionary. The originator was a man named Evara, who had apparently been given to seizures in his earlier days, before the cult was thought of:

"Whether the idea of the steamer and the returning ancestors originated here is not certain. But there was much talk at first of an aeroplane that was dropping messages from the sky.... Informants from Arihava told me (from hearsay) that Evara had in his possession a number of 'papers'—written messages that had come fluttering down from the sky during a feast in the village... Being questioned, however, Evara seemed altogether ignorant of the portent. He had no papers, he said, but there was a book in his box. This was immediately brought, and proved to be a modern novel of 244 pages—'Love and the Aeroplane,' with a very vivid portrayal on the cover of this kind of a machine, with a man and woman precariously attached to it by a rope." (p. 29)

In addition, on the wall of the *ahea uvi* of Evara's village was an advertisement for Lifebuoy Soap, "depicting a field-hospital, a motor ambulance, and a number of figures in uniform." All the figures were identified, one as Evara himself, and the others either as living persons or his deceased relatives.

The spread of the Madness is accounted for in two ways, the first by the "common method of...going to see" ceremonies and "then reproducing an imitation at home"; the second, by proselytizing. In this the Automaniacs were most active and came to have a great deal of power, so that "in certain villages, at any rate...it sometimes appears that they have superseded the chiefs." (p. 32) Their power was derived from an ability to divine and to heal; in the latter case, at least, they seem to have continued the older forms of extracting the object that "caused" a disease.

It is evident from this analysis that the Madness was a movement which, though of short duration, must have come with a tremendous surge because of the total situation of the natives in the face of domination by the whites. That it did not destroy as completely as is suggested seems to be clear; it is fortunate that the same student who was able to observe it so shortly after its inception was able in later years to return to the scene of his studies, and to make available a report of the manner in which the initial impulse was resolved.

g. Williams, F. E., *The Vailala Madness in Retrospect.*

This paper, written twelve years after the Madness began, shows how after the initial high enthusiasm which greeted it, the cult slowly abated until, with a final flare in 1931, its objectively discernible course was run. In retrospect, the author retains his original conclusions that "on the whole...not a few of the doctrines of the movement originated in visions and delusions; and it cannot be doubted that they were to some extent born of the mental confusion that followed the inrush of new European ideas." (p. 372)

Despite the failure of the specific events which were predicted to take place, the young people today show no tendency to regard the movement as a hoax, but hold "a widespread belief that the strange things which were expected to happen really did happen" so that "there still lives a popular belief that those first years of the Vailala Madness constituted a brief age of miracles." Three features are believed in with especial firmness; the coming of the phantom ship carrying the spirits of dead friends and relatives, the resurrection of the "boss" Ua Halai, and the matter of the ghost of Maivake.

As to the reasons for the appeal of the cult, we are told:

"...they are to be found in certain effects of contact with and subjugation by a superior people. Such contact involves (1) the effort to assimilate a body of new and difficult ideas, and a resultant mental confusion; (2) the loss of customary means of social excitement; and (3) a general sense of inferiority." (p. 377)

With regard to specific elements of the cult, it is shown how, for example, the flagpole as a carrier of messages from the dead developed from a knowledge of the radio station of the Anglo-Persian Oil Co., and in the case of each trait the rôle and importance of the leader in fixing the concept in the minds of his followers is analyzed, together with the manner in which the populace reacted to the "coming and going of credulity."

The author's conception of the wider significance of his research for students concerned with the processes of acculturation—a somewhat different point of view from those previously encountered—is well expressed in the following quotation:

"If the present paper has any claim to interest it is because it deals with a culture on the move. The Vailala Madness came as a violent shock to the societies of the Gulf Division, and the adjustment and reactions afford material for the study of culture in a state of unusually rapid metabolism.... It may be idle to speculate upon origins in a static culture; but there are more than enough native societies undergoing change at the present day, and the study of these has, I believe, a special importance, for here if anywhere we shall have a chance of discovering how elements of culture begin and how they grow." (p. 379)

4

In addition to the studies that have been analyzed, reference can also be made to certain other publications that consider the problems with which we are concerned.

A further important body of materials in the field of religion deals with the effects of acculturation among the American Indians as shown in the Peyote cult. In addition to the early studies of Radin, where he discussed the development of this doctrine among the Winnebago and presented sketches of the personalities concerned with its introduction and development in this tribe, there has been a considerable amount of subsequent research on the cult. Outstanding among these studies is that of Wagner, which in reviewing all the pertinent literature, not only treats of the acculturative development in specific tribes, but also analyzes the data from the point of view of the several impulses to be discerned in its movement from tribe to tribe, discussing the influence of each impulse in making for the variations in doctrine and ceremonialism that appeared as the cult spread.[1] One unusual recent paper belonging to this group describes a short-lived version of the cult as found among a group of Negroes who live in Oklahoma, in close proximity to the Indians from whom they obtained the Peyote religion.[2]

The considerable number of studies of New World Negro religious practices have largely been concerned with the carry-over of aboriginal African beliefs and rituals found among folk who are in the main professing Christians. To the historic control attainable in other acculturation studies, there is here added that further control which derives from an ability to assess the range of variation in a phenomenon subject to differing influences. For in the case of the New World Negroes, these groups, aboriginally endowed with a relatively homogeneous body of religious concepts, rituals and magical beliefs, were forced to undergo a series of contacts that differed not only as to severity of repression of African modes of worship, but also as to the forms of Christian doctrine and ceremonialism which were sanctioned by the whites of the various regions of their new abode., Hence the present-day religious life of Negroes can be compared in Catholic as against Protestant countries; while the question as to which tribal cultures are most represented in the survivals of African belief found in each region at the present time offers another salient for attack.[3]

The assimilation of new religious beliefs to old under acculturation has also received the attention of students in other parts of the

[1] Reference to Wagner's paper, as to all the others mentioned in these paragraphs, will be found in the list of works cited at the end of this book.
[2] Smith, M. G., (1934).   [3] Cf. Herskovits, M. J., (1930, 1935).

world; and this is especially the case, as far as native-white contacts are concerned, where missionary enterprise has been pursued with any degree of vigor. Except for studies aimed to facilitate the work of missionaries among folk who are bearers of the historic cultures of the East, however, data arising from this source tend to be of relatively smaller degrees of usefulness to the scientific student, since such material not only suffers from the handicaps which have been indicated when the relation of practical applications of anthropology to the scientific study of culture was discussed,[1] but also because of the fact that most of this work has been done by persons not trained in scientific anthropological techniques. And while the student of cultural contact can winnow much of use to him from these documents, for the most part materials of this sort must be employed with caution, since they are unavoidably conditioned by a point of view that has been restricted by the mandate under which students in this category have worked.

Something of the same point applies to acculturation studies in the special fields of political and economic life, for here most of the work has been done by those whose primary concern has been with the practical implications of their results for colonial administrators. In some cases, however, such as in the ethnological portions of the work by Brown and Hutt, data of scientific usefulness can be abstracted by students concerned with questions other than those confronting officials who must direct the course of native life during a period of change.

Though the same comments are valid for many studies of the effect of contact on social organization, there are some contributions which approach the phenomenon from the point of view of pure science, particularly the papers of Hallowell and Eggan. Both prove the widely held theory that social organization is less prone to change

[1] See above, pp. 29–32.

as a result of contact than any other aspect of culture to be untenable; moreover, they demonstrate that this change can be as profound as that in technology or any other phase of human civilization. And though they are not in agreement on certain other theoretical points, they are agreed that the changes which they have been able to control by careful recourse to historical documentation are phenomena of acculturation. In the case of the Abenaki studied by Hallowell these are ascribed to "the influence exerted upon Abenaki speakers by those of related Indian languages and Europeans,"[1] and in that of the Choctaw reported on by Eggan, to the contacts of tribes who "had a similar culture, resided in the same area, were removed to Indian Territory under similar conditions, and were subjected to similar influences while there."[2] The importance of the latter research is enhanced by the fact that it is one of the very few acculturation studies in which the contact of natives with natives is the sole concern.

The effects of acculturation on folklore are given explicit statement in but few studies. Painstaking investigations have been made by scholars working in historic societies into the manner in which themes from various sources have been combined in the tales of Indo-European peoples, but comparable analyses of such materials from primitive tribes are almost entirely lacking except as they have been done by American folklorists, and are available almost solely from American Indians and Negroes of the New World. Data in the first category usually consist of stories recorded from natives in which European motifs, and occasionally African motifs, can be discerned. Their elements are ordinarily not broken down so as to show how incidents of foreign derivation were worked into the aboriginal tales; still less information is available as to the relationship between these stories and their social setting. As these data, however, have that

[1] Hallowell (1928), p. 145.   [2] Eggan (1937), p. 39.

objective character which marks all folklore, their importance for the study of acculturation is of the first order.[1]

The work on New World Negro lore is characterized by more attention to provenience, while we also know more of the historical circumstances that brought about the folkloristic amalgam represented in the tales. In the main, however, the method used in presenting these tales is the conventional one of folklorists, wherein references are given to those folk from whom the same motifs have been collected. Much can be gleaned from this, however, concerning the manner in which these literary products have been subject to the process of repatterning and recombination that is so especially subject to observation in this field. The process is to be seen in the various collections from the United States and the Caribbean published by Parsons, in the Jamaican tales recorded by Beckwith, in the Bible stories collected from the Sea Islands of the Carolina Coast by Stoney and Shelby—though here the combination of elements needs no scholarly apparatus to make it apparent to the reader—in the intensive analysis of certain tales from Haiti by Comhaire-Sylvain, and in the stories reported from Dutch Guiana by M. and F. Herskovits.

The results of acculturation in the field of language have also received but little attention. Mention has been made of the comments in Mead's work on the "Antlers" regarding the English spoken by the Indians. Parsons also includes some remarks on the Spanish elements found in Zapotecan, referring to Radin's analysis of Spanish loan-words in that language. The problem, however, is one which touches all aspects of linguistic expression, and has to do particularly with the study of "pidgin" dialects. The approach to this problem developed by M. and F. Herskovits[2] recognizes the independence of the

---

[1] Examples of tales of this type are to be found in Thompson (1929) Ch. VIII and XI. References to most of the available collections of such stories are given in his Bibliography.

[2] (1937), pp. 117-135.

three aspects of language—phonetics, vocabulary, and grammar—
and holds that it is the last of these, and particularly that mode of
expression to which the word idiom is applied, that is the most
resistant to contact, while vocabulary is most easily worked into the
speech habits of those who must learn a new tongue. Analyzing the
various forms of Negro-English, it is thus shown how the turns of
phrase peculiar to all these dialects are to be referred to the fact that
in contact with the whites, Negro slaves learned the words of the
speech of their masters, and poured these words, which they pro-
nounced as well as they could in accordance with their aboriginal
phonetic patterns, into the mold of African grammatical forms. This
assumption is also valid for the speech of other New World Negroes, as
has been demonstrated by Sylvain's study of Haitian Negro-French.
That the same mechanism has operated in influencing English spoken
by natives of South Africa has likewise been indicated by Lestrade.

In those aspects of the aesthetic life comprising the plastic and
graphic arts and music, only a few studies bear on the processes of
acculturation. More suggestive than otherwise is the work of Lips, in
which he indicates the reactions of primitive people to whites by
reproducing their mode of portraying them. Most data having to do
with acculturation in the arts, however, are found in passing references
made by authors who, in the course of general ethnographic treatises,
speak of the manner in which European techniques have affected the
art of the folk whom they have studied. In the field of primitive
music Kolinski's analysis of the songs of the Bush and Town Negroes
of Dutch Guiana is perhaps the most extensive that has been made of
a musical idiom that is of known multiple derivation, but the studies
made by Herzog of the songs in the Ghost Dance rituals also indicate
how profitable data of this sort may prove to be for an understanding
of acculturation phenomena.

5

We may end our discussion of some of the available literature on acculturation on a non-scientific note, and consider what writers of fiction may give to scientists who seek to understand the results of culture contact, especially as these impinge on the lives of individuals who live under conditions of contact. To say that good ethnology is good art, and that to depict a culture so that it emerges from the pages in which it is described as the living entity it actually is needs the craft of the writer as well as the discipline of science, is merely to express something that has been sensed by many ethnologists, and acknowledged by some. The literary approach is particularly applicable in describing outstanding personalities found in primitive societies, as can be seen, for instance, in the biography of Chaka, the great military leader of the Zulu—a document that affords an insight into the character of its subject, and through this into the inner sanctions of the culture in which he lived, as does almost no scientific work on this or any related tribe.

In the situations of acculturation, where the stresses and strains on human personality are sharpened as a result of the confusion of cultures into which an individual is born, the freedom of the artist to throw the relevant material into sharpest focus should give the scientist many hints of value to him. One need only mention a few of the works of this kind that have appeared in past years to make the point; Freuchen's "Eskimo," for instance, with its portrayal of the results of the impact of white man's technology on Eskimo life, or Millen's "God's Step-children" and the light it throws on the life of the mixed Hottentot-Boer Bastaards of South Africa, or Williams and May's story of the experiences of the Kaffir, Shambala, in Johannesburg.

To give point to the remarks that have just been made, two of the more recent books of this type may be analyzed in the manner in which scientific works have been reviewed. In doing this, some of the points of significance in these books to be looked for in other fictional material of like calibre may be made patent to those who are concerned with that approach to the problems of acculturation that is termed scientific.

a. Smith, Bradford. *This Solid Flesh, a Novel of Intermarriage between East and West.*[1]

This novel tells of the change in Japan and in the attitudes of her people toward the western world and its ways in terms of the lives of four people: Yuki, married about 1870 to a warrior of the Samurai class who is killed soon after her marriage, and then to another of the type who was not unwilling to go along with the new commercialism; Masao, her son by her second husband, eager for the new knowledge, who comes to America and there, about 1905, meets and marries an American girl; Margaret, his wife, who bears her husband a daughter whose Eurasian status makes even more difficult the adjustments, at best anything but easy, that this American woman must make to Japanese life; and finally, Ruth, her daughter, who, torn between the conflicting claims of her dual heritage, finally breaks with the Japanese traditions and, as the book ends, marries an American and points her future toward life in her mother's homeland.

The tale not only treats with what appears to be great insight the personal problems of the Eurasian, thus throwing light on some of the aspects of their situation which must inevitably invade the personalities of such individuals, but in phrasing the reactions of the characters to the situations they must meet, and in placing them in their setting, many comments of value are given for those interested in the acculturative forces that have been playing on Japan since her contact with the Western World. Thus the reaction of Masao to life in his native country, seen after five years of study and work in the United States, is phrased as follows:

"Masao himself knew that a change was taking place. During the years in America he had almost forgotten how one did things at home. Yet it all seemed natural once he had returned. The leisurely, round-about way, the avoidance of all unpleasantness by courteous circumlocution came back to him and easily became part of his own practice....

"Business methods had been a shock to him, too. So many men working, such a leisurely air about the offices. Yet it was marvellous what had been done during his absence—the growth and improvement in the work of his company, the changing pace of Tokyo, the air of enterprise and confidence and progress. When he left, Japan had been a little country striving to be big; now it had become a nation conscious of its power and determined to increase it. He did not understand how old customs and new progress managed to exist side by side. Yet they did, and he had to fit them in together like everyone else...." (pp. 152–153)

There is much in this book of suggestion concerning the degree to which non-European cultures give way before European ones; it would seem that the author of this novel, who obviously knows Japan deeply and sympathetically, realizes that beneath the surface of Japanese life as it exists today, despite all its westernisms, the full stream of earlier tradition flows almost unchecked. This, perhaps, is the reason for the complete failure of Margaret to accommodate herself to the life of her husband's people though her desire might be ever so sincere and ever so strong, and of her failure to be accepted by them. In one place in the book she muses over her inability to understand Japanese modes of life:

"Often she asked about customs and events that interested her.... The answers were always hesitant, or contradictory if she asked them in several quarters, or not forthcoming at all. When sometimes in despair she suggested an answer the reply was always, '*So desho—*

Probably it is so.' Even Masao gave vague and unsatisfactory answers. Did it mean that they didn't know? Or that these things were secrets forbidden a foreigner? Often to her sensitive nature the latter seemed the case. Yet it appeared that certainty, logicality—call it what you would—was simply not important to a race which traced its social origins back almost a millenium before Christ. All these things were so because they were so; one knew them by intuition and destroyed them by explaining. Her way of thought and theirs simply did not match—hers the chain whose only virtue was in linking, theirs like a galaxy whose stars held together through no visible influence." (p. 156)

And again, when Masao and Margaret move into the European-style house they have built:

"Moving out of a Japanese house would, she felt, be a confession of her inability to enter its life—at least it would mean this for her. She had tried to enter and had failed—partly because a foreigner could never by a few years' residence, acquire the mental attitudes which had been forming through a hundred generations, and partly, she thought, because Yuki had not wanted her to enter and had not helped. Was there anywhere in the world another nation so homogeneous in blood, so purely of one stock that the whole population really felt themselves to be of a family? Of course they did not want her." (p. 201)

These excerpts are from that part of the book the action of which is laid about the year 1920. Ten years later, Ruth, Margaret's daughter, returns to Japan after attending college in the United States. Though expected to marry a Japanese who can be adopted by her father and thus, through her offspring, perpetuate the family in approved Japanese manner, she falls in love with Wayne, an American engineer residing in Tokyo, and eventually marries him. At a Japanese "party" given for a number of Americans who live in the city, he meets a geisha whose desire is to reform her calling and make of it the profession of entertainer. His train of thought further analyzes the problem:

"Here, while Ruth was up against the dictates of tradition, here in the heart of tradition were signs of change—a curious blending of Western morality with the old purposes of hospitality and entertainment, an attempt to embrace the new while preserving the old as Japan always did. And in this lay her strength. China, attempting the new, ended in chaos and revolution. Japan, through some secret chemistry, could blend without losing either flavor. So always behind the new customs and pursuits old ways of thought could be seen at work, and even in areas where tradition was strongest the new was welcomed, wherever it could improve. There was, after all, something symbolic in woolen underwear beneath a kimono, or in the neon light at the entrance to a brothel." (pp. 381–382)

Yet the old persists, and this is expressed when, near the end of the book, Masao reflects on the development of Japan since he went to America many years before as a young student:

"...He had hoped for a fusion of East and West, but though time had shown that foreign machines might run with equal efficiency this side of the world, tended by Oriental hands, foreign ideals had either to be adopted or dropped; there was no fusing them. All the progress in material things he had seen since his return more than twenty-five years ago—the unbelievable development of industry. the automobiles which, arriving shortly after his return, overran the city now, the inventions like his own which had brought the machine age to this quiet corner—this only made the difference clearer. One had but to scratch a surface anywhere in this corner of the world to find old metal underneath...." (p. 387)

b. McNickle, D'Arcy, *The Surrounded.*[1]

The fortunes of a half-breed Flathead Indian, Archilde Leon, are recounted in this story. At its outset he is found returning to the

---

[1] Copyright, 1936. The excerpts quoted here are used by the kind permission of the publishers, Dodd, Mead & Co.

reservation to visit his full-blood Indian mother before once more seeking the cities of the whites to find further employment. Circumstances hold him on the reservation, however, and he becomes reconciled with his Spanish father, at whose death he takes over the family property. His eventual entanglement in a situation that involves his presence at the murder of a game warden by his renegade brother and his complicity in hiding the crime, and his eventual attempt to escape punishment and the killing of the sheriff by the girl who accompanies him, are the major points of action which are woven into descriptions of situations and people which vividly portray the degradation of these Indians and the difficulties in any attempt to adjust their lives to the encroachments of white culture.

Two passages may be quoted; one indicates the official setting out of which this situation has developed, and the other the Indian's characteristic manner of meeting the outer demands of his new social environment:

"Mr. Parker, the agent, was a tall, active man whose hair was just beginning to grey. He liked his job and he liked his Indian wards. He saw their helplessness and realised, without getting excited about it, that he was of little use to them. He did what he could but at every turn he was hampered by a system which penalized initiative and by the Indians' own poor understanding of what was expected of them. Taking over an Indian Agency was always like moving into a ready-furnished house in which the pieces not only did not match but were falling apart and you had no authority to throw out anything or make better use of what was provided; and there were doors that led nowhere and some that would let you tumble into a dark cellar; the place was overrun by domestic animals which had to be fed and nursed, and you had no time for it if you were expected to keep the house from falling in on you; not a few of the pets had died before your time and others threatened to die, and altogether there was a bad odor around; the neighbors were always spying on you because, you at last realised, you were really in a house of prostitution and they were expecting you to add to its ill fame—in a word it was a nightmare which no one could endure without cultivating a certain amount of callousness. Above all, if an agent wished to remain in the Service, he had to keep his record clear. If in doing this somebody was put to an inconvenience or made to suffer, well—that was when it was handy to have developed a callous layer. Of course, if you were naturally fair, you tried to make it up in some way, off the record. In any case, whether you made amends or not, you had to be in the right position all the time. It was the only way to survive." (pp. 151–152)

The second quotation reads:

"There is a kind of chaos about an Indian's homestead that, however complete and hopeless, is nevertheless not inherent; it does not belong to the man. In the teepee, everything is in place; but when houses are built and farming implements acquired, then nothing is surprising; the hayrack stands before the front door and a mowing machine, with many parts missing, turns to rust; a wagon not far away is covered with an assortment of harness and saddles which never find their way to the barn; as there is no concentrated rubbish heap, tin cans are scattered to the yard at large; here are the ruins of some shade trees, sold and even planted by an energetic travelling nursery-man, but broken away limb by limb to provide whips for a lazy horse— they never had been watered anyhow, except by the dogs and a kind sky; a grindstone that has long ago jumped from its iron trestle lies fractured, one end of its rusty shaft obtruding, like the upraised arm of a drowning man; and these are only the few evidences of a foreign world." (pp. 195–196)

The tone of the book is consistently pitched toward descriptions of the more degrading aspects of cultural contact, and there is so little indication that new techniques and concepts have been worked into Indian life that the conclusion to be drawn is that experience with white culture has apparently not made for anything but disorientation. This may be the case; but it would also appear from the account of the manner in which the hero's mother, a life-long Catholic who before her death renounces the faith into which she had been baptized as a little girl and to which she had been so devoted all her life, that the tribe is rather living a life of passive resistance to forces more powerful than anything it can possibly cope with, until some adjustment to the present-day situation becomes possible.

III

SUGGESTIONS FOR FUTURE RESEARCH

I

A brief restatement of the approaches to the study of acculturation, and their importance both for problems of cultural dynamics and questions concerning the relation between an individual and his culture may now be given, together with some general methodological considerations.

The situations to be classed as acculturative fall into two categories. In one of these contact between peoples is a recent matter, and institutions are to be observed as they are in the process of reacting to the forces brought to play upon them. In the other the contact has taken place sufficiently long ago so that conflicts have been resolved and the present culture is a blend or a mosaic, depending on how far a harmonious consolidation of custom has been achieved.

The technique of utilizing the historical materials naturally differs in the two cases, as the ethnological approaches must differ. Where the contact is in process of continuation, its history is more readily recoverable than where the acculturative process was active many years ago, and in many instances this will make it possible to add to the testimony of documentary data information from those who were present at the beginning of contact. In the latter case the historical background will be more sparse, and such matters as information bearing on personalities who were active in the contact will be available only by a stroke of good fortune. As to the differences in method, the student who works in a society long acculturated can employ those devices conventionally used in studying "stable," "untouched" communities, since such folk will in all likelihood not be a great deal more variable in individual deviation from whatever norms have been set up after the amalgam was achieved than in "undisturbed" cultures. But this variation will be much greater where the accommodation to a foreign culture is actively proceeding, and hence the field method here must be flexible enough to allow for this.

Whether the work deals with one type of situation or the other, historic control can be exerted over the data, which means that in doing a study of acculturation the student is one step nearer an approximation of laboratory method than is possible where a culture is only studied as it exists on a single time plane, without any historical resources that can be called upon to document an otherwise unrecoverable past. This is to say that the study of acculturation offers the most favorable conditions for research into the nature and processes of culture because one is dealing with more known quantities than in any other type of investigation into the problems that challenge the student of human civilization. When cultures are in a state of flux, we can see happening, before our very eyes, the changes whose occurrences in societies that have reached a plane of cultural stability we can only postulate. And in dealing with the problems having to do with the reaction of culture on human personality, the situation of the individual under the conditions of cultural conflict that are in process of resolution tends to bring to the surface reactions to his cultural milieu that are so deeply submerged in less culturally turbulent times as not to be observable.

For the richest gain to accrue from research into acculturation, certain precautions must be observed by the student. That the greatest degree of objectivity must be constantly sought is a truism that would need no restating had not the failure to observe it been so richly documented in the preceding pages. The greatest possible alertness to the historic background of the folk being studied must be sought with equal consistency for, as may also be concluded from the foregoing pages, the degrees to which the historical resources dealing with a situation are exploited will be a measure of the degree to which a study can realize its potentialities. Above all, the student must be alive to all the factors; one party to the contact must not be approached with an *a priori* assumption of its greater significance than another; no group concerned in the contact may be neglected merely because on the surface it does not figure as largely as another; while, especially if the contact is between white and native peoples, it is not to be taken for granted that native civilizations must eventually give way before European or American culture. Otherwise the mind of the student will be closed to possible sub-surface developments that may be of far greater importance for a knowledge of cultural mechanisms—which is to say, of the propensities of human beings toward conservatism and change in their traditions—than much of what is overt.

An inevitable question that arises is whether the study of acculturation must lead to the formulation of laws of cultural processes. It is sometimes said that those who are interested in the historical relations between cultures and who insist on an historical approach to any study of cultural phenomena regard this as an end in itself, and feel that once the antecedents of a given situation have been analyzed, the aim of their research will have been achieved. This, however, merely represents a misunderstanding of the position of those who feel that consideration must always be given to the factor of time in the development of a culture, if that culture is fully to be understood.

History is essential; it is not enough. A scientific frame of reference must be present in the mind of anyone who makes even the most detailed research, if his research is to be of significance. Every scientist worthy of the name has an apperceptive mass of theoretical assumption, against which he is constantly projecting the data out of which he hopes, in the manner of any worker in science, to discover some principle that will enable him and his fellow-workers the better to understand the operations of the human mind as it manifests itself in those aspects of human group life we term culture. The study of acculturation is therefore only worth while insofar as it leads to a greater accumulation of fact, so that a resulting larger body of data will be available from which to draw conclusions. Because of its historic controls, it is a valuable additional weapon in the arsenal of the anthropologist; as such it should aid us in our search for an ever surer understanding of the operations of human civilization; but both the historical point of view and the generalizing frame of reference are essential.

2

It is apparent from the analyses of work in the field of culture contact that a first requirement is for studies to be made among peoples where the student can least identify himself with issues at stake. In terms of acculturation research, this means that the prime necessity is for investigation to be carried on among folk whose contacts involve no European or American group. A number of likely localities are available where the cultures cannot only be studied under conditions of contact, but in related forms prior to contact.[1]

One such area is that part of Africa that represents the southernmost extension of Mohammedan influence. In the region about Lake Chad, for example, pockets of Mohammedans are encircled by folk who have retained their pagan modes of life. Between these enclaves and their surrounding cultures there seems to be a constant give-and-

[1] An example of this kind of intertribal acculturation will be found in Herskovits (1938), vol. I, pp. 246–247, where the changes in form of the Yoruban Egungun secret society subsequent to its introduction into Dahomey—changes which bring its ceremonialism into consonance with Dahomean patterns—are set forth.

take that should be susceptible of revealing research. And this is equally the case in those centers of this region where Mohammedanism has taken firm hold, such as the cities of Northern Nigeria—Kano, Zaria, and the like. What of aboriginal custom persists? What of Mohammedan practice has been taken over? What amalgams of culture have resulted? Furthermore, this area offers the possibility that a series of groups can be ranged in accordance with their degree of response to the foreign body of tradition with which they have for varying periods been in contact, so that they can be studied in such a way as to employ and test the methods already employed in Mexico and South Africa. Similar studies of Mohammedan-native contact in process can also be made in East Africa, where Nilotic peoples are being constantly influenced by the Mohammedanized tribes to the north.

Another region where native-native contacts of this kind are available for study is Alaska, where Eskimo and Indian groups impinge on one another. Here a process of mutual borrowing seems to be resulting from this closeness of contact that is reflected in outer manifestations of the cultures of these folk; that concomitant change in inner values is also taking place is a reasonable presupposition that might be analyzed on the basis of the knowledge already on hand concerning the cultures which are contributing to the mixture. Central America offers still other opportunities for study of the results of contact between non-European peoples of different aboriginal traditions, in research that can be done among the Black Caribs of British Honduras. Unlike the preceding folk, these people, about whom to all intents and purposes no information at all is available, experienced their acculturation long ago, and therefore what might be studied would be that rarest of phenomena—the stabilized offspring of two known cultures, both on the primitive level. The entire problem of the results of Indian-Negro contact in the New World is as yet almost unprobed; and these peoples stand as an opportunity for any program of research that, though concerned with culture contact, seeks to escape from what on the surface appears to be situations inevitably limited to contacts between Europeans and natives.

In these regions—or wherever contacts between natives alone be the object of research—it is important that rounded studies which describe the culture as a whole be made, since work of this type will be pioneer work. Analyses of particular facets of culture are, of course, possible; the effect of Mohammedan-native contact on the magical practices of the aboriginal inhabitants of the West African area, and, on the other hand, the degree to which Mohammedanism as practised by these new converts is a deviant from the modes of worship officially sanctioned by this religion; the manner in which the technology of the Arctic dwellers of Alaska, both Indians and Eskimos, has been mutually affected by exposure to one another of different modes of adaptation to an exacting natural environment; the invasion of the linguistic habits of the Caribs by African patterns of speech. But though such special studies have undoubted value, it is preferable at present, when working with a people whose culture is as little known as are those that have been suggested, to lay the foundation for these more detailed analyses in the form of a presentation of the total culture as it exists, and in terms of its historical derivations, rather than to concentrate on specific aspects which cannot be satisfactorily understood until they are placed in their cultural matrix.

Another mode of escaping these ethnocentric temptations is for research to be done among peoples where the acculturation is between aboriginal folk and the historic cultures of the Far East. In the Philippines, Malaysia, Melanesia, and the Pacific Islands, contacts between Chinese, Japanese and British Indians, on the one hand, and indigenous folk on the other, are constantly making for the spread of these eastern civilizations to primitive peoples. The influence being exerted by the Japanese on the inhabitants of the Micronesian Islands at present mandated to Japan (provided that political exigencies permit such research to be carried on) offers a promising method for checking generalizations as to the results of native-white contacts. Is it true, for instance, that under Japanese control these natives, who are of the same stock as the Polynesians under British rule, show the same tendency to "psychological death" postulated by Rivers as a result of his study of the effects on them of contact with the outside, more powerful culture of Europe? Do they go through the same stages of accommodation to the culture of a "superior" people as Elkin has set forth on the basis of his research among the Australian aborigines? Similar investigation might also be made among the natives of Formosa, where Japanese rule has gone on for a longer period than it has in Micronesia; in any case, we have here a healthy means of recalling that native-white contact is only one of a number of comparable movements of vast geographical scope that are taking place at the present moment.[1] And in a similar way, analyses of the modes of life of other peoples who inhabit this area, where there has been a great deal of Chinese and British Indian penetration, would further check the statements of those who, quite outside the political sphere, have centered their attention too exclusively on contacts of Europeans and Americans with natives.

The suggestion made more than two decades ago by Radin concerning what may be termed the secondary results of acculturation which take the form of accelerated intertribal borrowing as a result of the imposition of a uniform outside control on a large number of aboriginal peoples should be followed by pertinent research. The compensations for loss of power made by tribesmen when they identify themselves with a native group larger than the older tribal

---

[1] An entire series of problems directed toward a similar end is available for study in the contacts of the primitive tribes of the U. S. S. R. with the European modes of life of the Russians. An example of how fruitful studies in this general area can be is to be seen in the analysis of Cossack-Tungus contact in Manchuria made by Lindgren (1938).

unit, as suggested in Mead's account of the "Antlers," is likewise worthy of study. Research of this kind will be oriented about two principal problems. The first of these requires the student to seek out and assess the levelling effect exerted by power brought equally to bear on a number of tribes, and the degree to which, as a result, the individual qualities of the separate cultures tend to be submerged in the characteristics which mark off the traditions of all the native groups taken as a whole, from the dominant culture. The second problem concerns the manner in which the opportunities for contact afforded under such conditions have resulted in intertribal acculturation—something that is quite different, as the preceding section has indicated, from the separate acculturation of each of the tribes in a region to the culture of the group that has sovereignty over all these tribes.

Four areas stand out as offering the most likely opportunities for studies of this nature—Melanesia, South Africa, West Africa, and the United States. In Melanesia, the effect of the recruitment of natives as laborers on the plantations offers a situation which should provide a fruitful field for studying the results that obtain when men of different tribes are thrown together over considerable periods of time. The same type of study—foreshadowed by the research of Hunter and more especially of the order of the approach employed by Hellman—is to be made in any of those regions of South Africa where natives are concentrated in considerable numbers. The Johannesburg mine compounds suggest themselves most immediately, but there are many other localities where a study of this sort can be carried on to advantage. In the seaports of British West Africa such as Lagos, Accra, and Freetown, native communities which number individuals belonging to all the tribes of the coastal area are found, and among these profitable research can be done. The mutual give-and-take that results when American Indians of many different tribes come together in rodeos and exhibitions of various sorts is well worth the attention of ethnologists. Such an obvious example of intertribal acculturation as the spread of the war-bonnet, now the authenticating label of a "true Indian" no matter what his tribe, comes to mind as a rough illustration of this sort of borrowing; but one can only speculate whether the obviously foreign elements seen in the performances of the various tribes of Southwest Indians at such a gathering as the Gallup Festival, assumed for purposes of show in the presence of a white audience, are carried home to invade tribal rituals.

No suggestions need be offered as to localities where acculturation between natives and peoples of European or American origin can be made, for such contacts constitute the majority of those now being investigated as well as the majority of those that have been studied. But in planning research among peoples who have experienced this type of contact, it might be the part of wisdom to seek to extend the scope of the bodies of data that have already been accumulated, rather than at the moment to seek out new regions where the effects of contact between whites and natives have not been studied. Four groups of cultures are thus indicated; in two of them contact occurred long ago, while in the other two contact is continuing. The valuable investigations that have been made of Mexican cultures should be continued by detailed research on more Mexican communities to show in what different ways the impulses begun by the early Spaniards have worked out. Similarly, further work on New World Negroes, which has also a broad basis of prior research among the Negroes of the United States, the West Indies, and South America, can throw more light on the impact of differing European traditions on the cultural heritage of the Negroes who were brought to the New World. In South and East Africa, the other two regions, analyses of the dynamics of culture-contact made while the phenomenon is occurring can also build on much prior work among these peoples; another advantage which would accrue to non-practical studies made here would be that they might furnish materials against which the scientific value of the results of studies made with practical applications in mind could be assessed.

In addition to these four regions, studies can also be profitably made among peoples whose pre-contact modes of life are known from the work of those ethnographers whose interest moved along the conventional lines of anthropological field-work of an earlier period of anthropological endeavor. Here the vast aggregate of data from American Indians should be of greatest service in supplying the student with background materials regarding the nature of the cultures of these tribes prior to contact; and a similar body of data is at hand for acculturation research in Melanesia.

3

Research concerning the effects of contact on specific aspects of culture also offers many opportunities to the student with special interests. Here, however, it is of importance again to emphasize what may appear obvious; that from the point of view of the best scientific strategy, such studies should be made where they can be based on previous rounded presentations of the entire culture of a people.

A few of these acculturation studies in restricted aspects of culture that can be based on materials at present available may be named. As has been said, studies of changes in political life and social organization under contact have received considerable attention from those concerned with practical applications of anthropology to the direction of native life, hence a principal objective of research done in these fields with no other than scientific ends in mind should be to check these other practical studies to determine their value as documents to be employed in studying the problems of pure science. In the field of the economic life of peoples who are living under contact, however, few studies have been published.[1] That the repercussions from the introduction of money into a non-pecuniary economy are wide-spread

[1] Cf. Firth, (1929).

is recognized by all who have dealt with situations in which this has occurred, and some attempts have been made to work out the resulting cultural realignments. In Africa alone such studies are needed from East Africa, where money was not used in pre-colonial times, and from West Africa or the Congo, where cowrie shells or iron, the aboriginal media of exchange, were replaced by European coinage. Studies of this type might also be made in Melanesia, where money-tokens were widely employed; in all such research, moreover, the influence exerted on other aspects of the culture by this new element in the economic life should constitute a principal end in view.

The fields of music and linguistics present many important problems for study. The manner in which musical idioms are influenced through contact is practically unknown, since the few available specialists in the field have been more than occupied with analyzing the forms of primitive music in the relatively few undisturbed versions that have been collected. However, such problems as the manner in which African musical styles have carried over into New World Negro music, and the degree to which these have manifested varying changes under contact with the differing musical traditions of Europe to which Negroes were exposed, present possibilities for research which carry a wider interest as they bear on current controversies as to the derivations of American Negro music. That similar problems are susceptible of study wherever two musical idioms have come together is evident; New World Negro music has been mentioned merely because of the variety of European musical traditions with which the African styles were brought into association, and the number of African and New World Negro songs that have been recorded and are thus available for study.

These same Negro peoples of the New World also offer great possibilities for the study of the influences of cultural contact on linguistic expression. Some materials are on hand, and what is needed at the present time are more data not only from the speech of the New World Negro peoples, but also information concerning the relationship between pidgin dialects elsewhere in the world, and the native languages on which they are based. Research is thus desirable into Melanesian and Chinese pidgin, into English as it is spoken in such a locality as Hawaii, into the Spanish of the Maya Indians and the French of Indo-China—at the very least, field-workers among such peoples, even though not linguists, should be encouraged to record texts in these pidgin dialects so that they can later be analyzed by specialists. It is also important that the English spoken by American Indian tribes be studied with the same point in mind, since the languages of many of these tribes have been thoroughly investigated, and texts of the various forms of Indian-English can be studied in the light of these aboriginal speech-patterns. Such research would be of great aid in testing the hypo-thesis of the results of linguistic contact that has been advanced in the preceding pages, to say nothing of testing the much older and more widely accepted thesis that holds such dialects to be merely expressions of the intellectual inferiority of non-European peoples who do not take over European languages in their pure forms. Re-search in the fields of folklore and religion may also be done along these lines, but it is not necessary, in the light of the preceding discussion, to detail either regions where such studies may be carried on or the problems that need special treatment, since these are evident both from the analyses of studies already made of the phenomena of contact as they affect these aspects of culture, and of the manner in which such problems may be attacked.

It remains, however, to mention one piece of research that, though not involving fieldwork, should nevertheless be of no little usefulness. Such research entails carrying much further the analysis of accul-turation made in this volume, by combing the literature to make available to students the enormous store of materials on acculturation to be found in works already published—a paragraph here, a casual

observation there, an *a priori* conclusion elsewhere—and by reworking this material so as to clarify the various statements that have
been made concerning culture contact, its mechanisms and results,
which, as we have seen, are in anything but agreement.[1] Research
of this kind would give a prominent place to the information concerning
the contacts of peoples to be found in the literature of travel and
exploration, especially that which deals with the discoveries of earlier
centuries. As a result, not only would all the data thus uncovered be
on hand for future students of acculturation, but the degree to which
contact has been a recurring and ever-present phenomenon in the life
of man would be made to stand out as sharply as its ubiquity merits.

4

The study of acculturation is equally of importance for those
concerned with the problems of the development of human personality
and of the interplay between personality and culture;[2] and if studies
of this type have received scant mention here, this has been because
to all intents and purposes they are non-existent. The psychologists
who deal with social phenomena have only in recent years come to
stress the force of culture in shaping the human psyche, while psychiatry has likewise tended in the main to overlook the importance of
the cultural factor. As far as attempts to bring these problems into
primitive societies are concerned, such studies of the development of
personality in primitive societies as have been attempted have been
made by anthropologists who, unfortunately, are anthropologists and
not specialists in the difficult field of the study of human personality;
while the very few such studies that have been attempted by those
competent to investigate the development of personality have lacked
the necessary anthropological background.

[1] Examples of material of this sort are to be found in such standard works as
Fletcher and La Fleche, Jochelson, Junod, etc.
[2] Cf. May and Doob (1937), pp. 1–2.

It has become so apparent that work along these lines among any of the primitive groups treated by anthropologists needs persons competent in the two fields concerned, that programs looking toward the training of personnel in both disciplines have been put forward and have received support in recent years. In the not too distant future, therefore, data of this order will be available in a proper setting and with interpretations that will be worthy of the most serious consideration both by anthropologists and others concerned with the development of personality, and the rôle played in this by culture. But when such research is instituted, those who command the necessary techniques will find that peoples who are undergoing acculturation, or who have passed through the stage but are still in process of resolving the cultural conflicts that have been inherited as a residue of contact, will have to be studied quite as much as those whose culture is more stable. For, as has been said, the influence that any culture exerts on its carriers is to be seen in sharper outline if studied in those situations where stresses are so accentuated that latent tendencies which might never come to the surface in more placid civilizations are revealed. Work in this dual field of approach among peoples such as the American Indians or South Africans, where contacts are continuing and tensions are sharp, will undoubtedly produce much that will be highly suggestive when compared with similar phenomena in more stable societies;[1] while in such countries as Haiti, where conflicting traditions have never been resolved, but have been so adjusted to one another that a mosaic has resulted rather than an amalgam such as is found in Mexico, materials of a similar sort should likewise yield a great deal of insight when studied in the light of findings from homogenous cultures.

---

[1] Since this was written, a volume giving in semi-fictional form the results of the psychoanalysis of a South African native who left his tribe to live in Johannesburg has appeared (Sachs, 1937). Its revealing quality should offer fresh stimulus to work of this type.

APPENDIX

Outline for the Study of Acculturation

by

Robert Redfield, Ralph Linton, and Melville J. Herskovits

I. Definition (*see above*, pp. 2–18)

II. Approach to the problem

    A. Listing of materials available for study.

        1. Published materials—of prehistoric contacts (to indicate how acculturation has characterized human contacts from early times), as well as contacts between primitive groups, between primitive and literate groups (both mechanized and non-mechanized), and between literate groups of either or both categories.

        2. Unpublished materials of studies in acculturation which are completed or in progress.

    B. Classification of the above materials

        1. Do these studies treat of entire cultures or specific phases of culture?

        2. If the studies are restricted ones, what phases of the culture are treated?

        3. What are the motivations of the studies (insofar as this affects the type of material treated); e.g., are they scientific, or are they designed to aid in the formulation of administrative, educational, or missionary policy?

C. Techniques employed in the studies analyzed
  1. Direct observation of acculturation in process.
  2. Recent acculturation studied through interviews with members of acculturated groups.
  3. Use of documentary evidence which gives historic testimony concerning early contacts that have resulted in acculturation.
  4. Deductions from historical analyses and reconstructions.

III. Analysis of acculturation
  (NOTE: The significance of physical type in determining attitudes operative in acculturation, as well as the importance of the concomitant occurrence of race-mixture or its prohibition, must not be overlooked as a factor which may pervade any situation, process, or result envisaged in this section.)

  A. *Types* of contacts
    1. Where contacts are between entire groups; or are between an entire population and selected groups from another population, e.g., missionaries, traders, administrators, special craftsmen, pioneers and their families, and immigrant males (all these considered with special reference to the elements of culture likely to be made available by the members of such special groups to the population among whom they live).
    2. Where contacts are friendly, or are hostile.
    3. Where contacts are between groups of approximately equal size, or between groups of markedly different size.
    4. Where contacts are between groups marked by unequal degrees of complexity in material or non-material aspects of culture, or both, or in some phases of either.
    5. Where contacts result from the culture-carriers coming into the habitat of the receiving group, or from the receiving group being brought into contact with the new culture in a new region.

society as influencing selection and acceptance of new traits.

2. As member of the donor group; personality of the individuals who are in contact with the receiving group, their attitudes and points of view, and the way in which the group to which they belong is regarded by members of the receiving group, as making for favorable and unfavorable reception of traits.

3. The individual as member of a special group in his society (priestly class, sib, secret society, etc.) and his position in this group, as accelerating or retarding acceptance of new traits.

B. Possible consistencies in personality types of those who accept or reject new traits.

C. Differential selection and acceptance of traits in accordance with sex lines, differing social strata, differing types of belief, and occupation.

D. Initial hostility and subsequent reconciliation of individuals to the new culture as a factor in integrating new culture-traits, and caused by

1. intensity of contact;

2. duration of contact and resulting habituation to new cultural elements;

3. social, economic or political advantages resultant upon acceptance;

E. Psychic conflict resulting from attempts to reconcile differing traditions of social behavior and different sets of social sanctions.

V. The *results of acculturation*

A. *Acceptance :* where the process of acculturation eventuates in the taking over of the greater portion of another culture and the loss of most of the older cultural heritage; with acquiescence on the part of the members of the accepting group, and, as a result, assimilation of them not only to the behavior patterns but to the inner values of the culture with which they have come into contact.

B. *Adaptation* : where both original and foreign traits are combined so as to produce a smoothly functioning cultural whole which is actually an historic mosaic; with either a reworking of the patterns of the two cultures into a harmonious meaningful whole to the individuals concerned, or the retention of a series of more or less conflicting attitudes and points of view which are reconciled in everyday life as specific occasions arise.

C. *Reaction* : where because of oppression, or because of the unforeseen results of the acceptance of foreign traits, contra-acculturative movements arise; these maintaining their psychological force *a)* as compensations for an imposed or assumed inferiority, or *b)* through the prestige which a return to older pre-acculturative conditions may bring to those participating in such a movement.

REFERENCES

Adams, Romanzo, 1937, *Interracial Marriage in Hawaii.* New York, Macmillan.

Anderson, H. D., and Eells, W. C., 1935, *Alaska Natives, a Survey of their Sociological and Educational Status.* Stanford U., Stanford Univ. Press.

Bartlett, F. C., 1923, *Psychology and Primitive Culture.* Cambridge (England), Cambridge U. Press.

Bateson, Gregory, 1935, "Culture Contact and Schismogenesis." *Man*, xxxv, No. *199*, 178–183.

——, 1936, *Naven.* Cambridge (England), Cambridge U. Press (see especially pp. 183–187).

Beals, Ralph, 1936, "Problems in the Study of Mixe Marriage Customs," in *Essays in Anthropology Presented to A. L. Kroeber.* Berkeley, Univ. Cal. Press.

——, 1937, review of "Mitla" by E. C. Parsons. *Am. Anth.*, xxxix, 681-682.

Beckwith, Martha, 1924, "Jamaica Anansi Stories," *Memoirs Am. F.L. Soc.*, XVII.

——, 1929, *Black Roadways, a Study of Jamaican Folk Life.* Chapel Hill, Univ. of N. Carolina Press.

Boas, Franz, 1896. "The Growth of American Mythologies," *Jour. Am. F. L.*, ix, 1–11.

Brenner, Anita, 1929, *Idols Behind Altars.* New York, Payson & Clarke.

Broadwood, Lucy E., 1907, "English Airs and Motifs in Jamaica," in Jekyll, W., *Jamaican Song and Story*, 278–285. Pub. of The Folk-Lore Society, LV. London, Nutt.

Brown, G. G., and Hutt, A. McD. B., 1935, *Anthropology in Action.* London, Oxford U. Press.

van Bulck, G., 1936, "De Invloed van de Westersche Cultuur op de Gesproken Woordkunst bij de Bakongo." *Kongo Overzee*, ii, 285–293, iii, 26–41.

Cator, W. J., 1936, *The Economic Position of the Chinese in the Netherland Indies.* Chicago, Univ. Chicago Press.

Chamberlain, A. T., 1902, "Earlier and Later Kootenay Onamatology." *Am. Anth.* (n. s.), iv, 229–236.

Chinnery, E. W. P. and Haddon, A. C., 1917, "Five New Religious Cults in British New Guinea." *The Hibbert Journal*, xv, 448–463.

de Cleene, N., 1935, "Les Chefs Indigènes au Mayombe. Hier, Aujourd'hui, Demain." *Africa*, viii, 63–75.

Comhaire-Sylvain, Suzanne, 1937 (see also Sylvain), *Les Contes Haitiens ;* 1 re partie, Maman d'l'Eau: 2e partie, Conjoint Animal ou Démon Déguisé. Brussels, Weteren; and Port-au-Prince.

Conzemius, Eduard, 1928, "Ethnographical Notes on the Black Carib (Garif)." *Am. Anth.*, xxx, 183–205.

Culwick, A. T., and G. M., 1931, "Culture-Contact on the Fringe of Civilization." *Africa*, viii, 163–170.

Dorsainvil, J. C., 1931, *Vodun et Nèvrose.* Port-au-Prince, Pierre Noël.

Dover, Cedric, 1937, *Half-Caste.* London, Secker and Warburg.

Ehrenreich, P., 1905, "Die Mythen und Legenden der Südamerikanischen Urvölker." *Supplement zur Zeitschrift für Ethnologie*, Berlin.

Eggan, Fred, 1937, "Historical Changes in the Choctaw Kinship System." *Amer. Anth.*, xxxix, 34–52.

Elkin, A. P., 1935, "Civilized Aborigines and Native Culture." *Oceania*, vi, 117–146.

———, 1937, "The Reaction of Primitive Races to the White Man's Culture," *The Hibbert Journal*, xxxv, 537–545.

Firth, Raymond, 1929, *Primitive Economics of the New Zealand Maori*, New York, Dutton (especially Ch. XIV).

———, 1937, *We, the Tikopia.* New York, American Book Co.

Fletcher, Alice C. and La Fleche, Francis, 1911, "The Omaha Tribe" in *27th Ann. Rep. Bureau of Am. Eth.*, Washington, Gov't. Printing Office (especially pp. 608–654; Appendix: "Recent History of the Omaha Tribe").

Fortes, M., 1936, "Culture Contact as a Dynamic Process." *Africa*, ix, 24–55.

Foster, Laurence, 1935, "Negro-Indian Relationships in the Southeast." Ph. D. Thesis, Univ. of Pennsylvania, Philadelphia.

Freyre, Gilberto, 1934, *Casa-Grande & Senzala.* Rio de Janeiro, Maia & Schmidt.

Gamio, Manuel, 1922, *Introduction, Synthesis and Conclusions ... The Population of the Valley of Teotihuacan.* Mexico, Sec. de Agriculture y Fomento.

Gayton, A. H., 1932, "The Ghost Dances of 1870 in South-Central California." *U. Calif. Pub. in Am. Archaeology and Ethnology*, xxviii, 57–82.

Gifford, E. W., 1924, "Euro-American Acculturation in Tonga." *J. Polynesian Soc.*, xxxiii, 281–292.

Groves, W. C., 1935–1936, "Tabar Today." *Oceania*, v, 224–240; vi, 147–157.

Haddon, A. C., 1935, *Report of the Anthropological Expedition to Torres Straits*, I, *General Ethnography*. Cambridge (England), Cambridge U. Press.

———, See also Chinnery and Haddon.

Hallowell, A. I., 1928, "Recent Changes in the Kinship Terminology of the St. Francis Abenaki." In *Atti de XXII Cong. Int. degli Americanisti* (Rome), 97–145.

———, 1936, "Psychic Stresses and Culture Patterns." *Am. J. Psychiatry*, xcii, 1291–1310.

———, 1937, "Cross-Cousin Marriage in the Lake Winnipeg Area." *Twenty-fifth Anniversary Studies, Philadelphia Anthrop Soc.*, Philadelphia, U. Pa. Press.

Harrisson, Tom, 1937a, *Savage Civilization*. New York, Knopf.

———, 1937b," The New Hebrides People and Culture." *Geographical J.*, lxxxviii, 332–341.

Hellman, Ellen, 1935, "Native Life in a Johannesburg Slum Yard." *Africa*, viii, 34–62.

———, 1937, "The Native in the Towns in the Bantu-Speaking Tribes of South Africa." In *The Bantu-Speaking Tribes of S. Africa* (Schapera, I., ed.).

Herskovits, M. J., 1927, "Acculturation and the American Negro." *Southwestern Pol. and Soc. Sci. Quarterly*, viii, 211–225.

———, 1928, *The American Negro, A Study in Racial Crossing*. New York, Knopf.

———, 1930, "The Negro in the New World: The Statement of a Problem." *Am. Anthrop.*, xxxii, 145–156.

———, 1934, "Race Mixture." *Encyc. of the Soc. Sci.*, XIII, 41–43. New York, Macmillan.

———, 1935, "The Social History of the Negro." In *A Handbook of Social Psychology* (C. Murchison, ed.). Worcester, Clark Univ. Press, 207–267.

———, 1936, "Applied Anthropology and the American Anthropologists." *Science*, lxxxiii, 215–222.

———, 1937a, "The Significance of the Study of Acculturation for Anthropology." *Am. Anth.*, xxxix, 259–264.

———, 1937b, *Life in a Haitian Valley*. New York, Knopf.

———, 1938, *Dahomey; An Ancient West African Kingdom*. New York, J. J. Augustin.

Herskovits, M. J. and F. S., 1934, *Rebel Destiny, Among the Bush Negroes of Dutch Guiana*. New York, Whittlesey House.

——, 1936, "Suriname Folk Lore." *Col. V. Contrib. to Anthrop.*, XXVII. New York, Columbia U. Press.

Herzog, George, 1935a, "Special Song Types in North American Indian Music." *Zeit. für Vergleichende Musikwissenschaft*, iii, 23–33 (Music, pp. 1–6).

——, 1935b, "Plains Ghost Dance and Great Basin Music." *Am. Anth.* xxxvii (1935), 403–419.

Hogbin, H. Ian, 1934, "Culture Change in the Solomon Islands." *Oceania*, iv, 233–267.

Holmes, W. H., 1896, "Pottery of the Ancient Pueblos." *4 Ann. Rep., Bureau of Am. Ethn.*, Washington, 265–358.

Hornbostel, E. M., 1926, "Review of Books on American Negro Songs." *Int. Rev. of Missions*, xv, 748 ff.

Hunter, Monica, 1933, "The Effects of Contact with Europeans on the Status of Pondo Women." *Africa*, vi, 259–276.

——, 1934a, "Notes on Changes in Xosa Resulting from Contact With Europeans." *Africa*, vii, 100–104.

——, 1934b, "Methods of Study of Culture Contact." *Africa*, vii, 335–350.

——, 1936, *Reaction to Conquest, Effects of Contact with Europeans on the Pondo of South Africa*. London, Oxford U. Press.

——, 1937, "The Bantu on European-Owned Farms." In *The Bantu-Speaking Tribes of South Africa* (I. Schapera, ed.) 389–404.

Hurston, Zora, 1931, "Hoodoo in America." *Jour. Am. F. L.*, xliv, 317–347.

Ichikawa, Sanki, 1930, "The Pronounciation of English Loan-Words in Japanese," In *A Grammatical Miscellany Offered to Otto Jespersen on his Seventieth Birthday*. Copenhagen, Levin & Munksgaard.

Ignace, Abbé Etienne, 1908, "Le Fétichisme des Nègres du Bresil." *Anthropos*, iii, 881–904.

Ishimoto, Shidzue, 1935, *Facing Two Ways*. New York, Farrar & Rinehart.

Jochelson, W., 1908, "The Koryak," vol. vi, pt. ii, *Rep. Jesup N. Pac. Exped.* (especially Ch. XIII and XIV).

Johnson, Guy B., 1931, "The Negro Spiritual: A Problem in Anthropology." *Am. Anth.*, xxxiii, 157–171.

Johnston, Sir H. H., 1910, *The Negro in the New World*. London, Methuen.

Keesing, Felix, 1928, *The Changing Maori*. New Plymouth, N. Z., Avery.

——, 1934, *Modern Samoa, Its Government and Changing Life*. Stanford U. Press.

Keesing, Felix M. and Keesing, Marie, 1934, *Taming Philippine Headhunters*. Stanford U. Press.

Kolinski, M., 1937, "Suriname Music." In *Suriname Folklore*, by M. & F. Herskovits, 491–758.

Kroeber, A. L., 1931, "Diffusionism." *Encyc. of the Soc. Sci.*, V, 139–142. New York, Macmillan.

Labouret, Henri, 1931, *A la Récherche d'une Politique Indigène dans L'Ouest Africa*. Paris, Éditions du Comité de L'Afrique Française.

Landtman, Gunnar, 1927, *The Kiwai Papuans of British New Guinea*. London, Macmillan (especially Ch. XXXIII, "The Pidgin-English of the Kiwais").

La Farge, Oliver, 1929, *Laughing Boy*, Boston and New York, Houghton Mifflin.

Lasswell, Harold D., 1935, "Collective Autism as a Consequence of Culture Contact: Notes on Religious Training and Peyote Cult at Taos." *Zeitschrift für Sozialforschung*, iv, 232–247.

Layard, John, 1936, "Atchin Twenty Years Ago." *Geographical J.*, lxxxviii, 342–351.

Lee, D. Demetracopoulou, 1936, "Folklore of the Greeks in America." *Folklore*, xlvii, 294–310.

Lesser, Alexander, 1933, "The Pawnee Ghost Dance Hand Game, A Study of Cultural Change." *Columbia U. Contr. to Anthrop.* XVI, New York, C. U. Press.

Lestrade, G. P., 1934, "European Influences upon the Development of Bantu Language and Literature." In *Western Civilization and the Natives of S. Africa* (I. Schapera, ed.), 105–127.

Lindblom, G. K., 1924, *Afrikanische Relikte und Indianische Entlehnungen in der Kultur der Buschneger Surinams*. Göteborg, Wettergreen and Kerber.

Lindgren, Ethel John, 1938, "An Example of Culture Contact without Conflict; The Reindeer Tungus and Russian Cossacks of N. W. Manchuria, 1929–1932." Forthcoming in *J. Roy. Anth. Inst.*, lxviii.

Linton, Ralph, 1936, *The Study of Man*, New York, Appleton-Century.

Lips, Julius, 1937, *The Savage Hits Back*. New Haven, Yale Univ. Press.

Lowie, R. H., 1935, *The Crow Indians*. New York, Farrar and Rinehart.

MacCrone, I. D., 1937, *Race Attitudes in South Africa*. London, Oxford Univ. Press.

MacLeod, William Christie, 1928, *The American Indian Frontier*. New York, Knopf.

Mair, L. P., 1934a, "The Study of Culture Contact as a Practical Problem." *Africa*, vii, 415–422.

——, 1934b, *An African People in the Twentieth Century*. London, Routledge.

May, Mark, A. and Doob, Leonard W., 1937, *Cooperation and Competition.* New York, Social Science Res. Council, Bulletin No. 25.

McKern, W. C., 1922, "Functional Families of the Patwin." *Univ. California Publ. in Am. Anth. and Arch.*, vol. xiii, 235–258.

McNickle, Darcy, 1936, *The Surrounded.* New York, Dodd Mead.

Mead, Margaret, 1932, "The Changing Culture of an Indian Tribe." *Columbia U. Contr. to Anthrop.*, XV. New York, C. U. Press.

Mekeel, H. Scudder, 1936, "The Economy of a Modern Teton Dakota Community," *Yale U. Pub. in Anthrop.*, No. 6.

Merick, G., 1908, "Notes on Hausa and Pidgin English." *J. African Soc.*, viii, 303–307.

Millin, Sarah Gertrude, 1925, *God's Stepchildren*, New York, Boni & Liveright.

Mooney, James, 1896, "The Ghost-Dance Religion and the Sioux Outbreak of 1890." *14th Ann. Rep. Bureau of Am. Ethnology*, part 2. Washington.

Morínigo, Marcos A., 1931, "Hispanismos en el Guaraní." *Univ. of Buenos Aires, Inst. de Filologia, Colección de Estudios Indigenistas, I.*

Moszkowski, Max, 1911, "Die Völkerstämme am Memberamo in Holländisch-Neuguinea und an den vorgelagerten Inseln." *Zeitschr. für Ethnologie*, xliii, 315–343.

Myers, C. S. 907, "Traces of African Melody in Jamaica." In Jekyll, W., *Jamaican Song and Story*, 278–285, Pub. of The Folk-Lore Society, IV. London, Nutt.

Nash, Philleo, 1937, "The Place of Religious Revivalism in the Formation of the Intercultural Community on Klamath Reservation." In *Social Anthrop. of N. American Tribes* (F. Eggan, ed.) 377–442. Chicago, U. C. Press.

Nekes, P. Herm., 1927, "Zur Entwicklung der Jaunde-Sprache unter dem Einfluß der Europäischen Kultur." In *Festschrift Meinhof.* Hamburg, 301–314.

Nina-Rodrigues, Dr., 1900, *L'Animisme fétichiste des Nègres de Bahia.* Bahia, Reis.

Ortiz, Ferdinand, 1917, *Los Negros Brujos.* Madrid, Editorial-America.

Park, Robert E., 1930, "Assimilation, Social." *Encyc. of the Soc. Sci.*, II, 281–283. New York, Macmillan.

Parsons, E. C., 1918, "Folk-Lore of Andros Islands, Bahamas." *Mem. Am. F. L. Soc.*, XIII.

———, 1923, "Folk-Lore of the Sea Islands, South Carolina." *Mem. Am. F. L. Soc.*, XVI.

———, 1928, "Spanish Elements in the Cachina Cults of the Pueblos." *Proceedings XXIII Int. Cong. of Americanists.* New York, 582–603.

———, 1918a, "Pueblo-Indian Folk-Tales, Probably of Spanish Provenience." *Jour. Am. F. L.*, xxxi, 216–255.

Parsons, E. C., 1918b, "Nativity Myth at Laguna and Zuni." *Jour. Am. F. L.*, xxxi, 256–263.

———, 1933, 1935, "Folk-Lore of the Antilles, French and English." *Mem. Am. F. L. Soc.*, XXV, parts 1 and 2.

———, 1936, "Mitla, Town of the Souls." *U. Chi. Pub. in Anthrop.* Chicago, U. C. Press.

Parsons, Elsie Clews and Boas, Franz, 1920, "Spanish Tales from Laguna and Zuni, New Mexico." *J. Am. Folk-Lore*, xxxiii, 47–72.

Peterkin, J. M., 1927, *Black April.* Indianapolis, Bobbs-Merrill.

Petrullo, Vincenzo, 1934, *The Diabolic Root, a Study of Peyotism, the New Indian Religion, among the Delawares.* Philadelphia, Univ. of Pa. Press.

Piddington, Ralph, 1933, "Psychological Aspects of Culture-Contact." *Oceania*, iii, 312–324.

Pitt-Rivers, G. H. L., 1927, *The Clash of Culture and the Contact of Races.* London, Routledge.

Powell, J. W., 1880, *Introduction to the Study of Indian Languages.* Washington, Govt. Printing Office.

———, 1894–1895, "Proper Training and the Future of the Indians." *The Forum*, xviii, 622–629.

———, 1896, "Report of the Director of the Bureau of American Ethnology for the year ending June 30, 1895." In *Ann. Rep. Smithsonian Institution .... to July, 1895.* Washington.

——— 1900, "Report of the Director." *19th Ann. Rep., Bureau of Amer. Eth. for 1897–98.* Washington.

Price, Maurice T., 1924, *Christian Missions and Oriental Civilization.* Shanghai, (privately printed).

Price-Mars, Dr., 1928, *Ainsi Parla l'Oncle... Essais d'Ethnographie.* Port-au-Prince.

Radin, Paul, 1913, "The Influence of the Whites on Winnebago Culture." *Proceedings of the State Historical Soc. of Wisconsin*, 137–145.

———, 1914, "A Sketch of the Peyote Cult of the Winnebago: A Study in Borrowing." *Jour. of Rel. Psych.*, xii, 1–22.

———, 1920, "The Autobiography of a Winnebago Indian." *Univ. of Cal. Publ. in Am. Archaelogy and Ethnology*, xvi, 381–473.

———, 1923, "The Winnebago Tribe." *37 Ann. Rep. Bureau of Am. Ethn.*, Washington.

———, 1930, "A Preliminary Sketch of the Zapotecan Language." *Language*, vi, 64–85.

Ramos, Arthur, 1934, *O Negro Brasileiro.* Rio de Janeiro, Civilizacaõ Brasileira.

——— 1935, *O Folk-Lore Negro de Brasil.* Rio de Janeiro, Civilizacaõ Brasileira.

Redfield, Robert, 1929, "The Material Culture of Spanish-Indian Mexico." *Am. Anth.*, xxxi, 602–618.

—— 1930, "Tepoztlan, A Mexican Village." *U. Chicago Pub. in Anthrop.* Chicago, U. C. Press.

—— 1932, "Maya Archaeology as the Mayas See It." *Sociologus*, viii, 299–309.

—— 1934, "Culture Changes in Yucatan." *Am. Anth.*, xxxvi, 57–69.

Redfield, R., Linton, R., and Herskovits, M. J., 1935, "A Memorandum for the Study of Acculturation." *Am. Anth.*, xxxviii, 149–152. Also in *Man*, xxxv, *162*, 145–148; *Africa*, ix, 114–118; *Oceania*, vi, 229–233.

Redfield, R. and Villa, Alfonso, 1934, *Chan Kom, A Maya Village*. Washington, Carnegie Institution of Washington.

Richards, A. I., 1932, "Anthropological Problems in Northeastern Rhodesia." *Africa*, v, 121–144.

—— 1935, "The Village Census in the Study of Culture Contact." *Africa*, viii, 20–33.

Rivers, W. H. R. (ed), 1922, *Essays on the Depopulation of Melanesia*. Cambridge (England), Cambridge V. Press.

Roberts, H. H., 1924, "Some Drums and Drum Rhythms in Jamaica." *Natural History*, xxiv, 241–251.

—— 1926, "Possible Survivals of African Song in Jamaica." *Mus. Quarterly*, xii, 340–358.

Sachs, Wulf, 1937, *Black Hamlet, The Mind of an African Negro revealed by Psychonanalysis*. London, Geoffrey Bles.

Sapir, E., 1934, "The Emergence of the Concept of Personality in a Study of Culture." *J. Soc. Psy.* , v, 408–415.

Schapera, I., 1928, "Economic Changes in South African Native Life." *Africa*, i, 170–188.

—— 1933, "Premarital Pregnancy and Native Opinion, A Note on Social Change." *Africa*, vi, 59–89.

—— (ed.), 1934, *Western Civilization and the Natives of South Africa, Studies in Culture Contact*. London, Routledge.

—— 1935, "Field Methods in the Study of Modern Culture Contacts." *Africa*, viii, 315–328.

—— 1936, "The Contributions of Western Civilization to Modern Kxatla Culture." *Trans. of the Roy. Soc. of S. Africa*, xxiv, part III, 221–252.

—— (ed.), 1937, *The Bantu Speaking Tribes of South Africa, an Ethnographical Survey*. London, Routledge.

Schrieke, B., (ed.), 1929, *The Effect of Western Influence on Native Civilizations of the Malay Archipelago*. Batavia (Java), Kolff.

Schuchardt, Hugo, 1914, "Die Sprache der Saramakkaneger in Suriname." *Verh. der K. Akad. von Wetenschappen*, Amsterdam, Aft. Letterkunde (n. s.), XV.

Schultze, Ernst, 1933, "Sklaven- und Dienersprachen (sogen. Handelssprachen)." *Sociologus*, ix, 377–417.

Seligman, C. G., 1929, "Temperament, Conflict and Psychosis in a Stone–Age Population." *Brit. Jour. Medical Psych.* ix.

Shonle, Ruth, 1925, "Peyote, the Giver of Visions." *Am. Anth.*, xxvii, 53–95.

Simpson, Eyler, N. 1937, *The Ejido, Mexico's Way Out.* Chapel Hill, Univ. N. Carolina Press.

Skinner, Alanson, 1916, "European Tales from the Plains Oji⸱⸱....] *Am. F. L.*, xxix, 330–340.

Smith, Bradford, 1937, *This Solid Flesh : A Novel of Intermarriage Between East and West.* Indianapolis, Bobbs-Merrill.

Smith, Mrs. Maurice G., 1934, "A Negro Peyote Cult." *J. of the Washington Acad. Sci.* xxiv, 448–453.

Speck, F. G., 1923, "Algonkian Influence upon Iroquois Social Organization." *Am. Anth.*, xxv, 219–227.

—— 1913, "European Folk-Tales among the Penobscot." *J. Am. F. L.*, xxvi, 81–84.

Spier, Leslie, 1921, "The Sun Dance of the Plains Indians: Its Development and Diffusion." *Anth. Pap. Am. Mus. of Nat. Hist.*, xvi, 451–527.

——, 1927, "The Ghost Dance of 1870 Among the Klamath of Oregon." *Univ. Wash. Publ. in Anthrop.*, ii, 39–56.

——, 1935, "The Prophet Dance of the Northwest and its Derivatives: The Source of the Ghost Dance." *Gen. Series in Anthrop.*, No. 1.

Stoney, S. G. and Shelby, G. M., 1930, *Black Genesis.* New York, Macmillan.

Sylvain, Suzanne, 1936 (see also Comhaire-Sylvain), *Le Creole Haïtien, Morphologie et Syntaxe.* Brussels, Wetteren; and Port-au-Prince.

Sutherland, I. L. G., 1935, *The Maori Situation.* Wellington, N. Z.

Thompson, Stith, 1929, *Tales of the North American Indians.* Cambridge (Mass.), Harvard Univ. Press.

Thurnwald, Richard, 1935, *Black and White in East Africa.* London, Routledge.

Todd, J. A., 1935, "Native Offences and European Law." *Oceania*, v, 437–460.

Torday, E., 1928, "The Influence of the Kingdom of Kongo on Central Africa." *Africa*, i, 157–169.

Vierkandt, Alfred, 1908, *Die Stetigkeit im Kulturwandel.* Leipzig, Daneker & Humblot.

Wagner, Günter, 1932, "Entwicklung und Verbreitung des Peyote-Kultes." *Baessler Archiv.*, xv, 59–144.

——, 1936, "The Study of Culture Contact and the Determination of Policy." *Africa*, ix, 317–331.

Warner, Lloyd, 1932, "Malay Influence on the Aboriginal Cultures of North Eastern Arnhem Land." *Oceania*, ii, 468 ff.

Walker, Abbé A., 1933, "Les Néologismes dans les Idiomes Gabonais." *J. de la Soc. des Africanistes de Paris*, iii, 300–314.

Westermann, Diedrich, 1934, "The African To-day." London, Oxford.

——, 1937, "Die Zukunft der Naturvölker." In *Lehrbuch der Völkerkunde* (K. Th. Preuß, ed.), Stuttgart, F. Enke. 383–404.

Williams, F. E., 1923, "The Vailala Madness and the Destruction of Native Ceremonies in the Gulf Division." *Territory of Papua, Anthrop. Report No. 4.* Port Moresby.

——, 1928, *Orokaiva Magic.* London, Oxford (especially pp. 3–101, "The Taro Cult, a Study of a Primitive Religious Movement").

——, 1933, "Practical Education: The Reform of Native Horticulture." *Territory of Papua, Anthrop. Report No. 14.* Port Moresby.

——, 1934, "The Vailala Madness in Retrospect." In *Essays in Honour of C. G. Seligman.* London, Kegan Paul. 369–379.

——, 1935, "The Blending of Cultures: An Essay on the Aims of Native Education." *Territory of Papua, Anthrop. Report No. 16,* Port Moresby.

Williams, J. Grenfell, and May, Henry John, 1936, "I am Black, the Story of Shambala." London, Cassell.

INDEX

"Place of Religious Revivalism in the Formation of the Intercultural Community of Klamath Reservation" analyzed, 85–90

Political life, studies of limited by "practical" ends sought, 105

Polygyny, incidence of, among Pondo under European contact, 68–69

Pondo, effects of contact on, 66–70

"Popular Science Monthly," early use of term acculturation in, 4

Powell, W. J., early uses of term acculturation by, 4

"Practical anthropology," 5
contrasted to scientific study of acculturation, 29–32
need for checking results in studies of by non-practical research, 125

Problems, for acculturation research, as bearing on relation between personality and culture, 129–130
in economics, 126–127
in European-native contact, 125–126
in folklore, 128
in linguistics, 127–128
in music, 127
in political life, 126
in prior literature on culture contact, 128–129
in religion, 128
in social organization, 126
in special aspects of culture, 122
involving no European peoples, 121–124
under intertribal contact, 123–125
methodological, in study of Haiti, 57–59

of Mexicans and American Indians, 45
of acculturation, areas for study of, 120 ff.

"Prophet Dances of the Northwest" analyzed, 76–82

R

Race-crossing, present interest in studies of, 1–2

Radin, P., 123
early acculturation papers by, 5
"Influence of Whites on Winnebago Culture," paper by, analyzed, 53–57
study of Peyote cult among Winnebago by, 1–3
study of Zapotecan linguistics by, 107

"Reaction to Conquest," analyzed, 66–72

Reconstruction of pre-contact cultures, difficulties of, 23–24
techniques of, 24
validity of objections to, 24–25

Redfield, R., 10, 131
quoted on analysis of culture into traits, 28
"Tepoztlan," work by, analyzed, 40–45

Religion, acculturation in, reasons for numerous studies of, 75–76
materials for study of, 103–104

Resistance, to European culture by Kxatla, 63–64

Revivalism, native, as contra-acculturative phenomenon, 75–76

Richards, A. I., 18

Rivers, W. H. R., 123
doctrine of disappearance of native peoples after contact with Europeans, questioned, 74